Affiliate Marketing for Beginners

From Side Hustle to Financial Freedom in 10 Simple Steps

Shane Finley

losses, direct or indirect, that are incurred as a result of the use of the information contained within this document, including, but not limited to, errors, omissions, or inaccuracies.

Table of Contents

Introduction

Have you ever thought about getting a passive or second income? Before you answer, you're probably wondering why I'm asking you that question, right? Let me explain. At the moment, many, if not most, people struggle to achieve financial security and financial freedom.

For the majority, their monthly expenses exceed income—as a result, they can't save enough for an emergency fund to cover any unexpected expenses. Also, they carry over credit card balances monthly and are more or less in a debt trap.

Major expenses like home rentals and medical expenses keep rising due to inflation and worsening global economic conditions. After the pandemic, many people lost their jobs, and many more have continued to live in a no-job-security state.

So, what about your situation? Do you think you have enough funds to save? This is why you need to think about a passive income option. According to my years of personal experience, affiliate marketing is one of the best options you have.

The cofounder of ClickFunnels, Russell Brunson, once mentioned, "Being an affiliate marketer is very cost-effective. You don't have to put much money in an affiliate program in order to gain a lot" (Convertful, 2019). According to him, the return on investment is high when you invest in affiliate marketing.

At present, affiliate marketing is a multi-billion global industry, and as of 2023, it has a market value of over $17 billion (Ruby, 2023). In addition, 8 out of 10 U.S. brands run an affiliate marketing program, and 16% of online orders in the country come through affiliate marketing (Mileva, 2023).

Additionally, the top affiliate networks have over 100,000 affiliates, with more male than female affiliate marketers (Mileva, 2023). Of the total affiliate marketers' population, the majority of their ages range between 35 and 44 (Digital Scholar, 2022). Moreover, 31% of affiliate marketers believe affiliate marketing to be one of their top 3 sources of revenue. As you see, you have the chance to tap into a higher income-earning bracket by also entering the affiliate marketing industry.

However, I have seen many people reluctant to enter this industry because they don't have sufficient information on the affiliate marketing process. That is the main reason I decided to publish this book is that I'm a professional marketer with a career spanning almost 25 years.

I worked in a variety of sectors, including engineering, tourism, and healthcare, before developing a passion for digital marketing. For the last 10 years, I have focused on building my own highly successful online business and have become an expert at selling other people's products and services via affiliate marketing. Currently, I live in North Carolina with my wife Chloe, my two children Eva and Jack, and my golden retriever, Florence.

Thanks to affiliate marketing, we now live the life we want. You also have the opportunity to create your dream life through the right affiliate marketing campaign. Why did I emphasize the word "right?" The first thing you have to remember is that affiliate marketing isn't a get-rich-quick scheme.

Your knowledge, experience, and skills will define you as a successful affiliate marketer. By reading this book, you'll learn everything you need to become successful in an affiliate marketing business.

The first chapter provides you with an overview of affiliate marketing. The second chapter evaluates the pros and cons of affiliate marketing. The third and fourth chapters cover the process of starting your affiliate marketing. In Chapter 5, we discuss the top affiliate marketing tools. Chapter 6 discusses the best affiliate marketing programs, networks, and examples. The final chapter caters to beginners, where I share certain tips based on my experience. So, let's begin your journey!

Chapter 1:

What Is Affiliate

Marketing?

Affiliate marketing: Have you heard this term before? Most probably, you might have seen headings marked affiliate links or sponsored posts on websites you visit. Nevertheless, affiliate marketing is a performance-based marketing process in which affiliates receive a small commission for each sale from marketing another person's or company's products.

Before we move into the complex topics, it's better to have an overall understanding of affiliate marketing. Therefore, this chapter aims to provide an overview of affiliate marketing. Main components and how affiliate marketing works will be discussed in the first part of this section. After that, types of affiliate marketing will be identified in depth.

Main Components of Affiliate Marketing

In the previous section, you might have wondered why I mentioned affiliate marketing as a performance-based marketing system. The reason is that you only get paid if your visitor takes action. In simple words, as a marketer, you promote a company's product or service through affiliate links. When a consumer purchases a product or service through your affiliate link, you earn a commission. In general, the commission will be a percentage of the sale price, or it can be a fixed amount.

In certain situations, you'll receive a commission for leads, free-trial users' clicks to a website, or getting downloads for an app. However, this depends on the affiliate marketing program and the company owner. You don't have any startup costs when starting affiliate marketing since most affiliate programs are usually free to join. There are four main parties involved in affiliate marketing, as follows:

- **Merchant:** The merchant is also known as the creator, the brand, the seller, the vendor, or the retailer of the product or service. The company size doesn't matter when you want to become a merchant; anyone can simply be one. In certain situations, the merchant does not even have to be the product or service creator, for example, Amazon Associates Program.

- **Affiliate marketers:** An affiliate, also known as a publisher, markets a merchant's product or service in an appealing way to potential consumers. Affiliate marketers can be either an individual or a company. In general, bloggers or content creators act as affiliate marketers, and they utilize their content such as blog posts, videos, email lists, or other media to promote merchants' products and services.

  Usually, affiliate marketers market products or services that are beneficial for customers, and they have a very specific audience. It helps them to create a defined niche or personal brand that convinces customers to purchase the product through their content. If the customer ends up purchasing the product, the affiliate marketer receives a commission.

- **The consumer:** Without sales, affiliate marketers can't earn a commission. In other words, to make a sale happen, there should be a consumer to purchase the product you promote.

- **The affiliate network:** In many situations, an affiliate network works as an intermediary between the affiliate and the merchant, but an affiliate network is not something compulsory. The majority of merchants choose to work with an affiliate network, to improve trust and reduce fraud rates because the network manages the relationship and provides third-party checks and balances.

Moreover, merchants are likely to work with an affiliate network due to the lack of time or resources to track, report, and manage payments to the affiliates. Sometimes, the merchant might work with multiple affiliates or publishers within the same affiliate network. ClickBank and ShareASale are the most popular affiliate networks (Lee, 2021).

How Does Affiliate Marketing Work?

As of now, we have an idea about the main components of the affiliate process. Let's identify the business model of affiliate marketing using a simple example. Let's assume you own a popular baking blog and YouTube channel which cater to a large audience. Then, one of the most famous electronic companies (ABC) contacts you about promoting their stand mixers and ovens on your platforms. Once you agree to work with them, you can show links to the ABC store on your blog or YouTube video descriptions (or anywhere else you've agreed on).

Once you sign up for an affiliate program, you'll receive a unique link that contains a tracking ID. This helps merchants to track whether customers come through your link. For anyone who clicks on your link, a cookie file will be stored on their device, and it holds an expiry date. As a result, when the customer makes an immediate purchase or if they purchased at a later date (before the cookie expiry date), you'll get paid.

Types of Affiliate Marketing

Before discussing the main elements of this section, let's consider the previous example. According to that, the blogger is recommending certain products of the ABC Company to their audience. How do you know whether they have used that product or not? Or whether they are simply promoting it for the money.

In some cases, such as skin care products, the customers may not trust an affiliate's recommendations unless they know that they have tested and approved the product themselves. To clearly identify affiliate marketers who are closely tied to a product or not, a famous affiliate marketer Pat Flynn (2018) categorized affiliate marketing into three types in 2009 as shown below.

Unattached Affiliate Marketing

Generally, affiliate marketing is a genuine business model which relies on reputation and the target audience's trust. However, unattached affiliate marketing is a bit different, and it can be considered an advertising or income-generating model. In other words, unattached affiliate marketing is the dark side or the most uninvolved form of affiliate marketing. Why is that?

In this type, affiliate marketers don't have any connection to the product or service they are promoting, or even with the end user. Also, they don't have any related skills or expertise in the niche or product. Because of that, they don't have any authority to make claims about its use.

Nevertheless, this method is popular among marketers due to the no-commitment factor. With unattached affiliate marketing, no product or customer relationship is needed. What they often do is just run pay-per-click advertising campaigns with affiliate links while hoping people will click and make a purchase. Personally, I don't recommend this method to anyone because it contradicts business ethics.

Related Affiliate Marketing

This technique is a happy medium between the unattached and involved. As the name suggests, here you promote the products or services that you don't use but that are related to your niche audience. And, make no claims about the use of the product or service. In this case, affiliate marketers typically have a larger audience on their platforms (blog, YouTube channel, social media, etc.) and are experts in generating traffic.

One of the main disadvantages of this method is the risk of promoting a bad product or service that you have never used before. Sometimes, that product may be related to your niche and the owner could be one of your best friends. Even so, if it's not the right product for your audience, you may lose the trust you built with them. For short-term-related affiliate marketing would be profitable, but in the long term, you won't be able to build sustainable affiliate marketing due to the lack of trust and transparency.

Involved Affiliate Marketing

As the name implies, the affiliate marketer recommends products and services that they used themselves and has the confidence and authority to make claims about their use. In this case, an affiliate marketer has a strong connection with the product or service they're promoting.

This method is truly based on trust and authenticity, as it draws upon an affiliate marketer's own time and experience to create a highly attractive offer for the target audience. In doing so, affiliate marketers have to uphold a high level of responsibility for the products or services they recommend to their followers.

This method is in stark contrast to unattached affiliate marketing because affiliate marketers use their reputation, trust, credibility, and authenticity to make money. They directly promote the products or services to those who may need them because they have confidence that their audience will benefit from the offerings.

Out of these three affiliate marketing options, this is the only type that can be truly described as credible, ethical, and sustainable. By now, I hope you have thought about which affiliate marketing type is most appropriate for you. In the next chapter, we will go deeper into why people go into affiliate marketing, starting with the advantages and disadvantages.

Chapter 2:

Why Affiliate Marketing?

Considering you decided to read this book, to begin with, there must be a part of you that is considering affiliate marketing as a potential income stream. You might be considering it as a part-time side hustle to your existing job, or you may be aspiring to do it full-time. Regardless of what your intention is, it's important that you fully understand the pros and cons of affiliate marketing. After we've covered this, we'll conclude with some frequently asked questions (FAQs).

Advantages and Disadvantages of Affiliate Marketing

Why should you do affiliate marketing? Here are the most prominent benefits of affiliate marketing.

Advantages

Easy to Execute and Scale

As I mentioned earlier, affiliate marketing is a business opportunity that you can start without worrying about the harder tasks like developing, supporting, fulfilling the offer, and so on. Simply put, you're supposed to handle only the digital marketing side of selling a product or service.

Then again, developing the right marketing skills takes a considerable amount of time and effort. Although that may be true, once you equip yourself with the right tools and find programs to work, you can easily tackle marketing any product in any niche.

Sometimes, you may feel you get a small portion of revenue from each sale as a commission. Believe me, still, you have the chance to generate more sales and reach higher income potential. There is an endless number of products or services to promote to your audience, and there is no earning limit for an affiliate marketer.

In particular, some brands, especially those with products that are difficult to market, offer 50%–70% commissions for promotion. The bigger your audience, the higher your earnings. It means affiliate marketing provides access to a broader market easily. For example, imagine you have a YouTube channel with thousands of subscribers. It's worth uploading a video by putting in your maximum effort because you have a bigger potential audience.

Also, you have the chance to promote complementary products apart from the main products. It helps you to extend your earnings. Even so, it's your responsibility to decide whether you conduct your marketing strategy as unattached, related, or involved. So, be mindful!

It's Passive Income and Provides Extra Sources of Income

When it comes to earned income, such as a job or self-employment, it requires you to put in the work to make money. However, affiliate marketing is a passive income method that enables you to make money while you sleep. Sounds interesting, am I right?

Once you work a certain period of time in your campaign, you don't have to put in the same effort afterward, and you'll be able to enjoy continuous returns. It helps you to have a steady flow of income. Also, you can maximize your returns by working on different affiliate programs at once.

No Customer Support Required

This is one of the main reasons many marketers choose affiliate marketing as their main source of income. Typically, sellers have to deal with their customers and ensure they are always satisfied. When it comes to affiliate marketing, you'll never have to be concerned whether the customers are getting enough support or whether they are satisfied with the product or service they purchased through your link. Your only responsibility is linking the seller and the customer. The seller has to take care of any customer complaints or after-sales services.

High Flexibility

As a result of the COVID-19 pandemic, many of us were required to work from home and, in doing so, got to experience the flexibility and improved work-life balance that working from home can offer. Affiliate marketing is the perfect business model for working from home—or anywhere you prefer that has an internet connection!

As an affiliate marketer, not only do you have the freedom to set your own goals and work your hours, but you also decide what products or services you want to promote, and the amounts, helping to diversify and maximize your income streams.

Low Risk and Low Cost

Normally, starting a business is risky because you have to allocate a huge amount of startup costs, and after that, you have to bear various costs such as employee salaries, rent, equipment, and utilities. With affiliate marketing, all you need is a platform to market. It can be your website, blog, YouTube channel, and so on.

That is why we call affiliate marketing a low-risk investment.

From the seller's perspective, traditionally, they would have to invest in marketing personnel or outsource to a specialist marketing agency, provide a marketing and advertising budget, and so on, all of which can result in significant overheads. However, if a seller hires affiliate marketers to promote their offering, they only have to pay the commission, which is much more cost-effective for them. This is also a win-win for affiliate marketers as the opportunities to generate income are more plentiful.

Drives Traffic Quickly

Affiliate marketing is one of the most effective methods to drive traffic because affiliate marketers utilize different approaches to promote products such as content marketing, blogging, YouTube, and social media marketing. Out of all these methods, blog posts are the best publishing method. Usually, Google ranks websites based on the number of backlinks, and building backlinks is a healthy approach to search engine optimization (SEO).

Let's assume the merchant hired a blogger as an affiliate marketer. Bloggers may include links in their content that directs to the merchant's website. As you see, it creates backlinks for merchants' websites, and it helps merchants to rank high in Google. Nowadays, merchants prefer to have more content like this, which, in turn, is a good opportunity for affiliate marketers.

Another possibility is when affiliate marketers post helpful product reviews and feedback on different platforms. This provides valuable insights for merchants. Merchants can use this information to improve their products and gain a competitive edge. Similarly, affiliate marketers also benefit from a more enhanced product via the commission from the increase in sales.

However, to write such an insightful review, an affiliate marketer must have a sound understanding of the product or service themselves, that is, they must have used it and be a fully involved affiliate marketer.

Facilitates Partnerships and Learning Opportunities

Typically, affiliate marketers sign up for multiple affiliate networks. In doing so, they are exposed to a wide range of people with expertise in different fields. The beauty of this is, you get to learn as you earn! Furthermore, there are countless products and services to choose from. So, don't stick to a particular product or service that you don't like. In other words, affiliate marketing allows you to do what you love most.

Disadvantages

Requires Patience and Hard Work

Let's be clear, as I mentioned in the introduction chapter, affiliate marketing is not a get-rich-quick scheme. It requires hard work and patience, especially in the early stages. If you're an absolute beginner, it will take time and effort to grow your audience and gain their trust.

Alongside researching credible products and services to promote, you'll also have to explore potential channels and platforms to reach your audience, not forgetting content creation! However, like most things in life, the greater the input, the better the output. Getting the basics right is key to creating a business that will continually deliver with minimal input from you.

Commission-Based and Unreliable Payouts

As an affiliate marketer, you don't have any control over the product or service, its quality, customer support, and so on. Similarly, you receive a commission based on the program's commission rate and the number of leads, clicks, or sales. So, you don't have any control over the payments, and you have no guarantee of the exact amount that you hope to gain through commission. Alternatively, there are common malpractices and risks in the affiliate marketing industry.

The first one is that some affiliate programs shut down without any proper notice, leaving the affiliate marketers unremunerated for the leads and sales they generated. The other one is that many merchants publish high payouts to attract affiliate marketers, but later, they gradually reduce them without any explanation. Therefore, it's important to choose the right product, merchant, and affiliate program after due diligence and proper research.

Highly Competitive

At the moment, the affiliate marketing industry is growing exceptionally, and it became popular as a passive income strategy for many people. As a result, thousands of people sign up for affiliate programs every day. It's evident that there is high competition, but that doesn't mean there are no opportunities for new entrants. The only way to beat the competition is to gain the right expertise.

Freelancing Is Not for Everyone

Some people enjoy their job, whereas others enjoy freelancing. Still, some freelancers feel lonely and stressed when they manage their workload themselves. To avoid these negative feelings, it's better to stay close to your loved ones. Additionally, you may think of going outside or to a designated remote working spot or renting a desk at a coworking space. All these strategies help you to build new connections, and your affiliate marketing will become more social and less stressful.

Risk of Building Another Business Instead of Their Own

In affiliate marketing, you work as a third party, and you don't engage with consumers directly. On the other hand, you're building someone else's brand instead of your own. Imagine you create an email list aiming to increase leads to sellers' websites. As a result, your visitors might visit sellers' websites instead of yours in the future.

Subject to Fraud

Like all other industries, there are also plenty of unethical activities happening. The most common one is providing fake leads and having fake followers. To avoid any kind of fraud or theft, affiliate marketers need to first be authentic. Also, merchants should properly vet any affiliates. They can check affiliate marketers' websites, social media platforms, and portfolios for anything suspicious.

Might Harm a Brand's Image

Brands must always remain transparent when it comes to affiliate activities. However, some brands don't disclose this information to their customers.

Conversely, affiliate marketers who don't comply with brand policies may damage a brand's image. To avoid these circumstances, it's necessary to inform the affiliate program, policies, and guidelines to publishers.

FAQs in Affiliate Marketing

It's best to clear most of the common questions you have before moving on to the upcoming sections. Here is a list of FAQs:

- **Is affiliate marketing legal?**

Affiliate marketing is legal. The affiliate marketer needs to report to their audience that they have a relationship with the merchant (BigCommerce, 2022). An example of a disclaimer is "ABC Company gave me the ingredients I'm going to use in this cooking video." This allows consumers to decide beforehand whether or not they want to continue watching and not feel like they've been tricked. It also helps them make an informed choice on whether or not to buy the product you're promoting.

- **Is affiliate marketing good for beginners?**

This is a good option for beginners since they don't require huge capital to start an affiliate marketing business. Even so, to become successful in this field, you're supposed to perform certain skills and expertise.

- **How much can affiliate marketers make?**

Affiliate marketers' income is limitless, but it can reach $100,000+ per annum. It will largely depend on the type of product(s) or service(s) you decide to promote, the type of affiliate marketing you adopt (unattached, related, or involved), relevance to your target audience, your reach, the time you invest in marketing, and so on. Like most things in life, the more you invest, the greater your return.

- **Can I start affiliate marketing with no money?**

Yes, there are multiple free platforms and affiliate networks that you can access for little or no money.

- **What are the best affiliate marketing products?**

There are countless products and services suitable for affiliate marketing. Regardless of which marketing strategy you opt for, ideally, you want to select products or services that have high demand and monetization potential, especially if you choose an unattached marketing strategy (BigCommerce, 2022). If you decide to implement a related or involved strategy, be sure to select products or services that you're genuinely interested in and are somewhat knowledgeable about. Remember, it will be easier to write about something that interests you than something that bores you to tears.

- **How do affiliate marketers get paid?**

Affiliate markets are paid a commission based on the commission rate of the affiliate program. Commission rates can vary from less than 1% to 20% or more. The amount you're paid will depend on the number of referrals you make. Payment methods, payment frequency, and so on, will be detailed in the particular affiliate program you register with.

- **What is the key difference between referral and affiliate marketing?**

Simply put, referral marketing incentivizes existing customers to introduce their family, friends, and contacts to become new customers, whereas affiliate marketing means third-party brand advocates promote the products of a retailer for a flat fee.

- **How can affiliate marketing help a retailer's business?**

Sellers can save time and money on marketing when they hire professional affiliate marketers. Also, it exposes its products to new audiences through affiliate marketing methods.

- **Can we have an affiliate program internationally?**

Yes, affiliate programs can be promoted in any country, but be mindful of the language.

- **What is a super affiliate?**

A super affiliate is someone who has built a thriving and influential affiliate business. As a result, their earning potential is high, which is usually in the range of five or six figures.

- **Is affiliate marketing still expanding?**

According to the statistics, affiliate marketing in the United States alone was $2.5 billion in 2012, $7.4 billion in 2021, and $8.2 billion in 2022 (Mileva, 2023). As you can see, affiliate marketing spend will continue to increase.

From what we've discussed so far, I hope you now have a better overall picture of affiliate marketing. So, what do you think about it? Are you satisfied with the benefits? I hope you're confident enough to embark on this journey and face any possible challenges head-on. Let's go.

Chapter 3:

How to Get Started in

Affiliate Marketing

So far, we've discussed the how and the why of affiliate marketing. In this chapter, we discuss the first six fundamental steps you should take on your affiliate journey.

In the first place, we identify how to choose a niche and the right platform. We then discuss how to build an audience and sign up for an affiliate program. After, we discuss how to choose products to promote and create remarkable content.

The journey to becoming an affiliate marketer can seem overwhelming at first. But if you break it down into smaller achievable tasks, you'll definitely reach your destination more easily. So, let's walk through each step.

Step 1: Research Your Niche

A niche is a highly specialized market that includes a focused set of people or businesses that are aligned with your specific products or services. Moreover, they need your product the most and are most likely to convert. Organic face wash or batik dresses are examples of niche products. Rather than focusing on an entire product catalog, you can start by honing in on one product that seems promising.

Similarly, instead of focusing on all kinds of clothing, you can specialize in batik and even narrow it down to female dresses. Some of you might think that having a niche means you have less chance to connect with as many people—it's actually quite the opposite. Here are the benefits that you can gain from focusing on a particular product or service, instead of a wide variety of offerings.

Focusing on a highly targeted, small audience means you have fewer buyer personas to consider when making decisions. Instead of a broader affiliate marketing strategy, a targeted strategy saves your marketing and advertising budget. Aligning your products with a specific group of customers helps you to have positive reviews and encourages customer loyalty. As a result, your social proof and word-of-mouth will be enhanced.

In particular, social proof refers to a psychological and social phenomenon where decision-making becomes credible and validated through the behavior of others (Dynamic Yield, n.d.). Social proof is now one of the main reasons why people are more likely to read blogs or share a link to your site—since they see others have already purchased your product or service. Furthermore, when you publish quality content based on your expertise consistently, it improves your SEO, helping consumers to find your website easily.

Similarly, customers will find your site reliable, reinforcing your credibility and authenticity as a specialist. It establishes brand recognition, grows expertise, and builds authority. Generally, mass markets often evolve from niches. So, you have the potential to become a long-term business one day. Starting small today means building the foundation for the future. Let's discuss how to find a niche market, starting with knowing your passions.

Know Your Passions or Interests

As you already know, you have to create plenty of content to succeed in affiliate marketing. If you choose something you hate, there is a possibility of you giving up in the middle of the journey. When you choose an occupation you enjoy, it will never feel like work. So, start by making a list of all your pastimes or skills you're passionate about or good at, then analyze each item carefully. Here is a list of questions to help you brainstorm:

- What am I good at?

- What do I like doing?

- What topics do I really enjoy learning about?

- What topics am I already passionate about?

- What unique experience do I have?

- How do I like to spend my free time?

- What am I curious about?

- What do other people tell me I'm good at?

- What perspective can I offer that my competitors can't?

- What industry is my business or brand in? How is it different from others?

- Do I already have experience or training in a specialized area?

Once you answer these questions, you'll be able to identify your core strengths, and you'll be amazed by the number of potential niches you get. If you don't have any hobbies or skills that go in line with a niche, you have the option to recruit niche specialists, or freelance writers to produce your website content.

In this case, you don't need to know much about the niche, but you have to think about the long-term cost you have to bear. Google Trends, Answer Socrates, and Exploding Topics are the most popular niche research tools that you can utilize to extend your research.

Diagnose the Problems and Needs of Your Customers

In this stage, you have to decide whether your passion or interest meets your customers' needs or problems. One of the best methods that you can use here is customer buyer personas and market research. Those methods help you to determine the buying behaviors and challenges of customers, as well as give you a better idea of how your business can provide value to your niche market.

A buyer persona is a fictional profile that reflects a particular target customer. Google Research, Census Bureau, Make My Persona, Tableau, Paperform, and Statista are the most popular tools and resources for conducting market research.

Identify Monetization Opportunities Within the Niche

Cofounder of NP Digital, Neil Patel, once said, "There's no point in getting into affiliate marketing if you can't monetize it, and you can't drive traffic and sales. You'd just be spinning your wheels" (Convertful, 2019). As he indicated, there is no point in selecting a niche if you can't generate profits, and if you can't drive traffic and sales.

So, it's wise to choose a niche that has several monetization options; you'll then have multiple income streams, which reduces your risk. First, identify what monetization methods your competitors are using. Subsequently, Google your primary topic and analyze the top 10–15 websites that appear in the results. Typically, these are the sites that need to be monetized with sponsored content; for example, Google Ads and Amazon products.

Thirdly, go to Amazon and discover which product affiliates can promote in the niche and identify the products that are suitable for your audience. Likewise, you may use other affiliate networks, such as ClickBank, Commission Junction, and OfferVault to evaluate the profitability.

Product quality, price, customer location, demographics, customer values, and interests are the main things that should be considered when it comes to product features. Most importantly, check whether you're comfortable enough to recommend products to customers. Amazon, agency directories, G2, and Pricefy are the tools that you can incorporate to analyze competitor pricing and determine prices for your products and services.

Research the Competition and Search Volume for the Niche

The main purpose of this stage is to identify how many other businesses you'll be competing with and whether the niche itself can make you money. So, don't confuse niche analysis with keyword research. Semrush is a good tool that you can use here. Once you type the broad keyword on it, it will display the other keywords related to your niche.

There are some other features that help you to have detailed research. Keyword difficulty reveals how hard ranking for a keyword is, whereas cost-per-click (CPC) shows how much money, on average, marketers are prepared to pay for one click of a keyword. The search volume indicates how many times people search for a keyword on Google.

It's a good idea to find keywords with a CPC of $2 or more and a minimum search volume of 10,000. These figures reflect that the retailers are willing to pay a considerable amount to display their ads for these search terms. Also, if your niche has a high CPC, it means you have the potential to generate substantial returns.

AnswerThePublic, Exploding Topics, Google Trends, Ubersuggest, Google Keyword Planner, ClickBank, and Amazon are the research tools that you can utilize in this stage. Keep in mind, it's best to avoid the niches that have little competition because your profit potential is limited.

Moreover, it's better to evaluate volumes and the possibility to scale. For example, first, take a broader niche like fashion and use it as your primary keyword. Next, use several sub-niches such as dresses, shirts, shoes, accessories, and jewelry to see which keyword combination has a higher search volume.

Do not forget to examine the business' scalability and how you can improve your product, content, and affiliate marketing strategies in your selected niche. After that, analyze the possibilities of adding new products, categories, promotional platforms, or opportunities for partnerships in the longer term.

Gauge the Diverse Range of Traffic Sources Available

Usually, good affiliate marketers don't depend on one traffic source. On the other hand, a niche affiliate platform that has limited traffic sources typically has lower growth potential. Therefore, as an affiliate marketer, it's important to have multiple traffic sources to have a stable online presence. Mainly, what you can do here is look at the top websites in your proposed niche and evaluate where they get their traffic from.

For example, you might notice social media is the main source of search engine traffic for a particular website. After that, analyze each platform—whether it's Facebook, Pinterest, or Instagram. Likewise, you can expand your research to have detailed insights.

SimilarWeb is one of the most useful tools for researching the traffic sources of different websites.

Before you conclude your decision, identify how you can stand out from the crowd. So, you may analyze competitors' content and list the problems within it. Secondly, evaluate how you can do better than them. For example, you may include unique content, videos, images, some case studies, and detailed examples. Hopefully, by now, you'll realize that finding a niche is not as tough as many believe. Nevertheless, be cautious to find a niche that is worth entering. Here are the top niches for affiliate marketing:

- fashion

- beauty and cosmetics

- health and wellness

- food

- home decor

- gardening

- travel

- education

- technology

- gaming

- finance

- art

- pets

- sports

- luxury

Step 2: Choose the Right Platform

With a niche in mind, the next step is to decide on the platform to publish your content. Here are the most popular types of platforms for affiliate marketing:

- websites

- social media

- YouTube

- newsletters

- podcasts

The type of platform you select mainly depends on your preference and your niche's preferences. Let's assume you're planning to publish content about playing tennis. Videos will be the most effective option to share your content, and YouTube will be the best platform to publish them. Also, it would be great if you could have a website as well. Use SEO to rank your content high on Google.

This technique helps you to generate passive search traffic, and have consistent clicks on affiliate links. The Federal Trade Commission requires you to be transparent when receiving income. Therefore, don't forget to disclose the fact that you're including affiliate links in your content despite the platform you use.

Step 3: Build an Audience

Having a large audience who read, view, and engage with your content is highly important to increase your income. Once you establish your audience, ensure you build trust and credibility with them. It helps you to turn them into loyal customers. Always give them a purpose or reason to refer to your content, and, gradually, they will find a reason to buy your recommended products as well. Let's discuss how to create a loyal audience with affiliate marketing.

- **Be aware of your target audience:** The first thing you have to do is identify your target audience by analyzing your competitors and traffic. For example, if your niche is related to cake-making, your audience will most likely be young adults. Accordingly, use effective advertising methods to target that particular age range

- **Be trustworthy:** As we discussed earlier, a key objective of an affiliate marketer is to generate income. However, the content you create must provide value for your target audience. If your audience senses you're trying to take advantage of them, they will likely avoid your content in the future. So, when creating content, make sure to be transparent, honest, and truthful.

  Similarly, check whether the products or services you promote are relevant to your chosen niche and audience. As a best practice, you can create personalized and professional links by shortening URL links. It helps you to improve the possibility of clicks and commissions from sales.

- **Experiment with programs:** No rule forces you to stick to only one affiliate program for the long term. If your chosen affiliate program is not working, you have the freedom to shift to a different program and try various opportunities. Affiliate programs differ, offering a wide variety of products and services. It's not always necessary to join a large program.

  Sometimes, you may think of trying a small program. Do not think testing out multiple programs and doing your research is a waste of time. Various programs allow you to collect more information on affiliate marketing.

- **Paid promotion:** You can use paid promotion to market your content, and Google Ads and Facebook promotions are the most popular options. It does not always have to be a paid promotion. Instead, you can cross-post your content on different platforms to maximize exposure.

- **Stay relevant:** No one likes to refer to outdated content. Make sure to be up-to-date with the current trends, news, and your affiliate program. Accordingly, you'll be able to identify new ad units, products, and tools to help you update your content, and maximize your traffic and commissions. Always predict what your target audience is looking for and deliver it to them through your upgraded content.

Step 4: Sign Up for an Affiliate Program

An affiliate program refers to an agreement or partnership in which a business pays another business or affiliate marketer a commission for sending traffic or sales their way. This can be achieved through multiple ways, such as social media channels, web content, or product integration. An affiliate program is one of the best ways to start affiliate marketing.

Once you sign up for an affiliate program, you'll get an affiliate link that contains a unique ID, and you can include those links in your content. Affiliate links also use cookies to track clicks, and whether the users made a purchase. Each cookie has a length or cookie life. That period refers to how long the cookie will track the user's online activity.

For example, if the cookie's lifespan is one month, your user has to buy the product or service within one month of clicking your affiliate link for you to get paid. If the time expires, a lead will no longer be trackable.

In general, there are no upfront costs to join an affiliate program, and you may simply look for products or services you and your target audience may like or be interested in. However, there can be variable ongoing costs based on how you want to promote the products and services to your potential customers. When selecting an affiliate program, consider the platforms or avenues where your audience spends the majority of their time.

As an example, do your buyer personas usually research new products by scrolling through Facebook or reading blog posts? Do they look for a good deal or promotions on a site? Or, are they doing tons of research before finalizing their purchase decision? Let's go through the types of affiliate programs:

- **Search affiliates:** In this type of program, marketers usually pay their own money to promote affiliate offers on search results. Sometimes, it can be other online advertising platforms like Facebook Ads.

- **Influencer programs:** These types of programs are especially suitable for bloggers or social media influencers. Typically, they have a specific audience; therefore, they can consider partnering with another company. Let's assume you're a travel blogger or YouTube influencer. So, you may think of partnering with a company that sells camping items. If they agree to partner, then you can feature their products in your content by including an affiliate link in exchange for a commission.

- **Review sites:** At the moment, the majority of consumers research and refer to other customers' reviews before making any purchase. Therefore, review sites play a huge role here. Most of the review sites are paired with individual companies or affiliate networks to review products and services in exchange for an affiliate link.

- **Coupon sites:** This is somewhat similar to the previous category, and coupon sites partner with merchants to provide buyers with discounts on products and services in exchange for an affiliate link.

- **Email marketing:** I have seen many people sending bulk emails without having a proper idea of who's receiving them. From my point of view, it's an ineffective method, because, sometimes, your emails might be received by someone who isn't interested in promoting products or services. So, it's better to send emails to users who may be interested in your content.

  For instance, imagine you work for a marketing agency. Then, you can partner with a company that sells design tools. When you contact your clients through email, you may include affiliate links for design tools in your content. In this case, you're delivering high-quality content to your clients while having an added source of revenue.

You can find affiliate programs by searching on Google or referring to affiliate directories. Or, you may check the relevant company's website. Let's identify a few factors you should consider before you sign up for an affiliate program. First, consider how suitable the affiliate program is for your niche. For example, if your niche is organic food, it will be counter-productive to promote beauty products to your audience.

Do not underestimate the value of promoting the right product to your audience. Promoting the wrong product will diminish your authority in that niche. Also, it gives a bad impression to your users that you're not capable enough to help solve their problems. So, be mindful to research and find out whether the chosen product is relevant to your audience.

It's wise to select a product you know or have used before. Once you identify an appropriate product for your niche, then determine how best to promote your affiliate link. Your promotional channels will differ depending on your product of choice. For instance, the way you promote products in the entertainment niche is totally different from the products in the healthcare niche. However, some affiliate programs have certain terms regarding promotional activity.

For example, some affiliate programs don't allow their users to run a campaign on Google targeting some keywords. Hence, before you sign up for an affiliate program, check whether you have the freedom to use your preferred promotional channels. YouTube videos, email campaigns, social media, and blog posts are the most popular methods of promoting affiliate links.

As an affiliate marketer, not only are you promoting another business' product or service, but you're also simultaneously building your brand. You only want to select and promote a business with a strong brand reputation, as it will positively impact your brand through association. Take the time to thoroughly analyze your chosen affiliate program. Not only do you want to register with a program that offers competitive commission rates but also one that will also enhance your reputation.

Imagine you earned a huge commission, but their payment method is not supported in your country! Be sure to check out the payment methods provided by a particular affiliate program before signing an agreement. Some affiliate programs also operate a payment threshold, meaning you have to earn a minimum commission before it's processed for payment.

The minimum payment can range from $50 to $200 depending on the program. For instance, with the ConvertKit affiliate program, there is no minimum payout, whereas, for ClickFunnels, you have to earn at least $100 in commission before you can get paid.

Another important thing to consider is cookie shelf life, as it can hugely impact your potential to generate commission. As we discussed earlier, every cookie is valid for only a certain time. The longer a cookie's shelf life, the greater your potential to earn a commission. Cookie shelf life ranges from 0, 45, 60, 90, to even 120 days.

To effectively promote your chosen product or service, you need certain tools such as videos, images, written reviews, different banner sizes, or email swipe copy. So, all these tools are known as affiliate kits. Likewise, check whether your chosen affiliate program is supportive and whether they assign an affiliate manager who will assist and guide you when you encounter challenges.

Also, make sure to refer to the terms and conditions in the agreement to be clear with the rules, guidelines, and restrictions that you must adhere to as you join an affiliate program. Last but not least, check whether the affiliate program offers a system to track sales. The best affiliate programs will be introduced in Chapter 6.

Step 5: Choose Products to Promote

Once you have chosen your niche, audience, platform, and affiliate program, this is the time to select a product or service accordingly. I have emphasized the factors related to this section many times. Here is the summary and a few tips on how to choose which affiliate products to sell. It's always best to choose a product that you've used before, as well as products that you're familiar with and confident in. Also, don't directly tell anyone to purchase a product.

Make sure to recommend the products based on your experience and in the context of what you have done. You must, I repeat must, choose products that fit within your niche. As well as check whether your core values align with the company's core values. Likewise, analyze whether chosen merchants value affiliate marketers and their effort.

I have seen some helpful merchants who provide tools such as banners, product images, and demographic information to their affiliate marketers. If you're starting out in affiliate marketing, these tools can prove very beneficial in getting you up and running.

Most importantly, check whether your chosen merchant is recognizing your affiliate link and whether they utilize tracking functions appropriately. In particular, partner with successful people in the affiliate marketing industry. They might help you with product selection and provide valuable information about the latest products, the best traffic sources, and higher commission rates.

I have observed that most people tend to promote the same products by following the crowd. However, if you investigate your niche thoroughly, you'll be able to find some hidden gems. In certain situations, choosing the right product can be very tricky and frustrating. Still, it's a prerequisite factor to succeed. So, be patient and select the right fit for you as well as your targeted audience.

Step 6: Create Remarkable Content

None of the previous steps matter if you don't have original, informative, and high-quality content where your affiliate links fit naturally. Do not just blindly place affiliate links in your content. Creating effective content that resonates with your audience is a must to help them to make an informative decision on a product or service and to boost your site's performance on search results.

It increases organic traffic and helps you to attract new visitors. Therefore, content writing plays a major role in this stage. Content writing is the process of writing, editing, and publishing content in a digital format. Let's dive into the types of content for your affiliate marketing:

- **Product reviews:** According to recent statistics, 97% of consumers look at online reviews before visiting the site and purchasing any product or service (Costa, 2021). Authentic reviews will be appreciated by the audience—so, make sure to include the actual experiences you had with the product or service you recommend.

- **Product comparisons:** These are quite similar to product reviews. Here, you may place similar products and highlight the pros and cons. In this category, you don't have to point to one product. Hence, you may promote multiple products and include several affiliate links in your content.

- **Product roundups:** This is somewhat similar to product comparisons. Instead of comparing products, you can recommend different brands for different purposes or include complementary products within the same category or theme.

- **Tutorials:** This is an effective method of highlighting how the product or service works through a step-by-step process. Customers are inclined to trust and purchase a product or service when they exactly know how it benefits them.

- **Emails:** If you have an active and engaged audience, emails are the best option to promote your affiliate brand. You can highlight the product features as an educational series, or you can include affiliate links in a particular section of the email. Email is also a great way to make your readers aware of the other platforms that you use to publish content.

- **Ebooks:** Sometimes, you won't be able to explain a topic in-depth via a blog or email. Ebooks would then be the ideal option to cover any comprehensive content. Unlike other types of content, ebooks need a lot of effort and time to create. Nonetheless, once you create it, it acts as evergreen content which benefits you in the long term.

  For instance, if you're a beauty influencer, you can publish an ebook about the beauty topic you specialize in. You can promote products or services, and add affiliate links in the ebook. Moreover, an ebook is an ideal way to build your email list by requesting recipients to share their email addresses in exchange for the ebook download.

- **Landing pages:** You can direct users to dedicated landing pages from your other platforms such as social media posts, email, and ads. You can use the landing page to include more information about the product and service and convince consumers to buy. In addition to that, you can add a link that directs to your ebook, a video, and so on. As best practice, don't include too many links to other resources to avoid distracting the reader. Your primary goal is to get your reader to click on the affiliate link.

- **Case studies:** This is another effective method, and these can be published as blog posts, YouTube videos, dedicated landing pages, and so on. It's best to include as much information as you can. Start describing the challenges. You can then present a product as the solution. Finally, you can highlight the benefits to really make the content compelling.

- **Resources pages:** Also known as pillar pages, they gather all the significant information and content around a specific topic from a range of websites, including your own. You can include a resources page in a blog or a website and include all the helpful links, educational articles, resources, tools, videos, and content in one place. This is a great method to establish your authority as an expert.

- **How-to articles:** These are some practical articles that show various ways to do something; for example, how to write an attractive blog post. In the middle of the content, you can add relevant affiliate links.

- **Guides:** Similar to how-to articles, with these, you can use your content to educate people in a specific area comprehensively; for example, a guide to better online brand awareness. Usually, guides will be longer. So, it's best to research your chosen area before you publish the content as a guide. Ensure to provide information regarding credible industry statistics, best practices, user reviews or expert opinions, and so forth.

- **Listicles:** As the name implies, these are the articles that provide helpful lists; for example, top skincare routines, or the 20 best holiday destinations you must visit. Here, you can include multiple affiliate links based on the affiliate programs you take part in.

- **Seasonal content:** As the name suggests, you publish according to different holidays and times of the year; for example, Christmas Day, Mother's Day, New Year's, and so forth. To be more effective, check the calendar ahead of time and identify the opportunities to publish something people will be looking for via your content.

The majority of affiliate marketers write their own content. So, I thought sharing a few tips on how to take your content to the next level would be helpful. Writing unique and original content is fundamental to publishing quality content. Start by researching your topic. Keep in mind that simply copying and pasting from Google is not enough.

What I personally practice is to first prepare a rough outline, based on my research. I then start working on the content. Usually, 60% of the content is based on information from online research, and the remaining 40% from personal examples, original anecdotes, or tips.

If I don't know much about the topic, I reach out to experts or refer to their original publications. Sometimes, I reach out to my social network to find a reputable source who is willing to share their original examples, tips, or quotes. I also refer to other social media platforms such as LinkedIn, YouTube, Reddit, and Quora, to enrich my content.

If your audience can readily access content akin to yours on Google, why would they bother with your content in the first place? So, my advice to you is to go above and beyond to take your content to the next level. It will reward you in the long run.

Realistically, you're not going to have huge enthusiasm or passion for every topic you write about. You might not even find it remotely interesting. However, you still should remain determined to create quality content.

Remember, your reputation and credibility with your audience are at stake.

In these situations, you need an awesome hook and an attention-grabbing introduction. There are techniques that can help you with this. For example, start with a well-known quote and explain how it directly impacts the reader. Present your content in a manner that will keep your reader engaged. Avoid text-heavy content and aim to make it highly visual by embedding imagery or video or including blockquotes.

When creating high-quality content, your ultimate goal is to convert users into prospects and, ultimately, customers. Therefore, it's imperative that you include strong calls to action (CTAs) where relevant and drive traffic to click on your affiliate links.

There are no hard-and-fast rules to publishing content, but it's best to be precise and concise, and not overly descriptive. From experience, I find that readers generally don't like to rely solely on their own thoughts and opinions but prefer a more rounded approach where insights, facts and figures, and examples from experts are also provided.

This will help build trust and credibility with your audience. Be mindful when creating content that you're not writing just for the sake of it. Rather, you should always have your audience in mind: What pain points are you trying to solve for them, and how can your content add value for them?

Don't forget to edit your content once you finish. Make sure not to publish repetitive, redundant content full of fluff. Check whether there are any grammatical or structural errors. If you're not competent enough to do this, you might want to consider hiring a freelance editor. Being an SEO-savvy writer helps to rank your content high on whichever platforms you're publishing.

Hence, it's great if you can learn key SEO tactics and incorporate them into your content. You should also give due consideration to understanding the nuances of your chosen platforms and how content reaches and inspires your audience on them. Having an awareness of any unique platform features will help improve the quality of your content.

Best-selling author and keynote speaker, Andrew Davis, once said, "Content builds relationships. Relationships are built on trust. Trust drives revenue" (Marinaki, 2021). This quote can be considered a summary of what we have covered so far. Ultimately, your content should be able to build relationships and trust. Gradually, readers will convert into consumers, which generates that all-important revenue.

If content writing isn't your strongest point, don't worry, there are plenty of resources to help get you started. Start learning and become an expert in content writing to become successful in affiliate marketing. Listed below are free online tools and resources that you can refer to as you start your content creation journey.

Usage	Tools and Resources
Content research	<ul><li>Google Trends</li><li>Ahrefs</li><li>HubSpot Blog Topic Generator</li><li>Google Scholar</li><li>AnswerThePublic</li><li>Google Docs Explore tool</li><li>Google Search</li><li>Percentage Change Calculator</li></ul>
Content writing	<ul><li>Blog templates</li><li>CoSchedule's Headline Analyzer</li><li>Evernote</li><li>OneLook Thesaurus</li><li>TitleCase</li><li>Lose the Very</li></ul>

	• WordCounter • Word2CleanHTML • HubSpot Free CMS
Content editing	• Grammarly • HubSpot Marketing Hub • Hemingway Editor • Editorial calendar templates • StackEdit • WebFX Readability Test
Designing tools	• Google Fonts • Canva • Infogram • Nimbus Screenshot & Screen Video Recorder • Skitch

	• Infographic templates
	• Image Color Picker
	• HubSpot's Free Stock Photos
	• Placeit
	• LICEcap
	• ICONS8
	• PowerPoint templates
	• Haiku Deck
	• Noun Project
	• SlideShare templates
Productivity tools	• Trello
	• Coffitivity
	• Giphy Search
	• TomatoTimers
	• OneTab

If you have successfully reached this part of the book, you should now be able to determine your niche, platform, target audience, affiliate program, product or service to promote, and how to create quality content. In the next chapter, we explore how to build momentum and achieve sustainability in affiliate marketing.

Chapter 4:

Build Momentum and Achieve Sustainability in Affiliate Marketing

You may consider this chapter as the second part of the previous chapter, since we will discuss the remaining four steps involved in building an affiliate marketing strategy. We will, firstly, explore how to drive traffic and those all-important clicks on your affiliate links. Afterward, we will discuss how to track the performance of your affiliate campaigns and how to increase sales, and look in detail at the payment structure of affiliate marketing. Let's start with driving traffic to your site.

Step 7: Drive Traffic to Your Affiliate Site

First off, if you have been actioning the steps as you've been reading, you'll now have created awesome content. The next challenge is to get your content in front of your audience. In other words, how to drive traffic to your site. Here are some tips to consider.

- **Have realistic goals:** You probably are well aware of the income potential from the likes of TikTok and YouTube videos. However, it's difficult to guarantee the long-term effectiveness of such content. So, don't depend on get-rich-quick methods on social media. Instead, have realistic expectations, put in the work, and be patient.

- **Choose the right niche:** It's tempting to choose your niche based simply on income potential. However, highly lucrative niches tend to also be highly competitive with lots of affiliates promoting the same products. Ideally, you're looking for that sweet spot where a product or service is in demand, but the competition is relatively low.

- **Capture emotional triggers:** Generally speaking, people tend to base their buying decisions on how it makes them feel and then

60

justify their spending with logic. When creating content, be sure to consider emotional triggers; how would the product or service make your audience feel, look, and so on? The more you can tap into their emotional triggers, the greater the likelihood of your audience clicking on your affiliate links.

- **Know your target audience:** To have a better understanding of your customers, you should have a good idea about their pain points, emotional triggers, needs, and wants. It's best if you can be close enough to your target audience to get more insights into how they think and feel. When we analyze customers' pain points, we generally consider only the solution to a problem. Hereafter, make sure to be concerned about the symptoms of the problems as well, to have a complete understanding.

- **Be cautious with paid advertising:** It's true, paid ads are the fastest way to drive traffic to your links. However, volume is not everything. You must also consider the quality of traffic. If the traffic being generated is not interested in your product or service, they won't click on your affiliate links, and you'll have wasted both your time and money. Understanding your target audience and selecting the correct keywords are paramount in ensuring you invest your money wisely.

The below list, in no particular order, has the best traffic sources for affiliate marketing:

- paid traffic

- blog posts

- SEO

- YouTube

- Facebook

- Pinterest

- TikTok

- email marketing

- Quora

- ebooks

- giveaways and promotions

- product reviews

- guest blogging

- link placement

- reputation management

Step 8: Get Clicks on Your Affiliate Links

By now, you should have a sound understanding of affiliate links and how they work. Let's take a closer look. There are five main parts to an affiliate link (Lent, 2021):

- **Affiliate tracking domain:** "A domain set up by the affiliate network which forwards your user on to the brand or advertiser."

- **Affiliate identifier:** This part of the affiliate link "identifies you as the affiliate sending the referral."

- **Merchant identifier:** This "identifies the merchant receiving the referral."

- **SubID:** This is "customizable text you can use to track which content and links are driving the best conversions."

- **Deeplink:** This indicates the exact advertiser's website page you want to send the visitor to; for example, the homepage.

Where and how you place affiliate links in your content is critical to ensuring your audience clicks on them. You want to avoid looking like a complete spammer by placing all your links in the introductory paragraph. Likewise, you want to avoid placing links at the bottom of your content, as users are unlikely to scroll that far.

Getting the balance is key; inserting links early without overdoing it is what you're aiming for. You also want to ensure the links are in the same context as the rest of your content and flow seamlessly. Imagine you're going to publish the best travel packages under $1,000. If you place links as follows (imagine there are hyperlinks on the bold parts), they look out of context and spammy:

> Today, **I'm** going to introduce **the** best **travel packages**.

If you mention your introductory sentence below, it would make more sense:

> Today, I'm introducing 10 different travel packages you can purchase from ABC Travels for under $1,000. These are **package name 1**, **package name 2**, and **package name 3**.

As you see, this is more clear and more effective than the previous example. Furthermore, you can include callouts like eye-catching boxes, buttons, and tables that can help attract your readers' attention and make the post more skimmable.

Let's look at some other ways you can create high-converting content.

- Ensure links in your body text are easily identified by underlining and changing the font color. Blue usually denotes a link, but you can use any color.

- Avoid using naked links which can look messy and not very readable, ensure your affiliate links use anchor text, which is in context to the topic and informative for your audience. This will also help with your SEO.

- Insert CTAs in highly visual buttons with your link.

- Embed links into imagery.

- For product reviews, comparisons, and so on, include charts and tables to make your content more appealing and digestible for your audience.

- When appropriate, employ a scarcity tactic to aid conversion. For example, limited-time offers, seasonal offers, and low-stock notices.

Step 9: Track Your Affiliate Campaigns

Out of all the above-discussed methods, how can you check what works for you? Or, which aspects of your online activity produce the most traffic, conversions, and clicks? This is why you need an effective affiliate links tracking strategy. In addition to that, affiliate tracking boosts affiliate management productivity and saves money plus time.

Moreover, the majority of affiliate tracking techniques offer deep research details to have a better grasp of your target audience and advertising networks. Similarly, you can optimize your campaign since a variety of tracking methods, live reporting, and analytics tools allow you to measure various key performance indicators (KPIs) and generate accurate data.

Based on this information, you may choose the best affiliate marketing partners and can identify your largest buyer's audience. Correspondingly, you can design an extensive campaign by including new ways to present your products. Overall, affiliate tracking helps you to maximize your affiliate marketing income. There are different types of affiliate marketing tracking methods such as cookies, SubID tracking systems, and impression tracking.

As an advanced step, you can incorporate affiliate marketing software to monitor the traffic and conversions. Before you select software, check whether they offer multiple tracking options such as offline tracking, action tracking, per-product tracking, and lifetime commissions. Software flexibility is another feature that you must look into. In other words, tracking software should be able to change by default, and it must enable you to customize your platform when the network expands.

On top of that, evaluate whether the affiliate marketing tracking system provides up-to-date fraud detection features and precise reports. Sometimes, you may need customer support when setting up or while operating. So, before you make your purchase, check whether you get after-sales services. You may analyze software providers' customer support availability and responsiveness through their customer reviews. Here is a list of affiliate marketing tracking software platforms.

- Everflow.io

- AffTrack

- Impact.com

- CAKE

- Post Affiliate Pro

- OSI Affiliate

- TUNE

- LinkTrust

- HitPath

- ClickInc

- Voluum

- FirstPromoter

- AffiliateWP

Step 10: Increase Your Affiliate Sales and Get Paid

While the previous steps will guide you to start your own affiliate marketing campaign, this is the step where you learn how to generate revenue. Let's discover various strategies that you can implement to maximize your affiliate income.

Use KPIs to track your success: First thing we have to understand is that all the affiliate links don't generate income. That's the truth. So, instead of depending on vanity metrics, focus on the numbers that matter. You can keep your eye on the following metrics. Click-through rate (CTR) gives you an idea of the number of clicks in comparison to views.

You may use this KPI to evaluate the performance of the links, ads, CTA, and so forth. Conversion rates provide you with details of the number of conversions compared to the clicks. Conversions can be sales-related or any step you want your visitor to take, like signing up for a newsletter and downloading an ebook. You may use revenue by traffic source KPI to evaluate which of your platforms generate the highest income.

Additionally, you may determine which pages are valuable enough for readers based on the average time they spent on your page. Alternatively, you may utilize A/B testing to determine your best-performing content while incorporating a suitable KPI. Here are some tips:

- **Link to conversion-optimized landing pages:** Many people think clicks automatically translate to sales. Unfortunately, in reality, that's not the case. Your affiliate links should drive to the appropriate landing pages to increase the chances of generating more affiliate sales. For instance, when you discuss the most popular travel destination in your country through your blog, you can partner with a travel company to promote their travel packages. Once you're partnered, your affiliate links should directly link to the merchant's page where users can immediately purchase those travel packages.

  Another page you can easily generate sales with is your tools' webpage. You can link your tool list to conversion-optimized pages or other useful content like comparison articles or your own reviews. Do not forget to keep those pages up to date and easily accessible to your users. According to the statistics, it's evident that people tend to browse and shop in their native language (Affiliate Academy, 2023). Therefore, always try to drive traffic to localized sites. Users can select their preferred language through the language menu available on most of the sites. On the contrary, some companies have different sites, for different countries, for example, Amazon Affiliates.

- **Highlight reviews:** It would be tough to introduce a new product or service to your target audience at the beginning. So, to persuade your clients, you can back up your recommendations with reviews from other happy customers or third-party review sites such as G2 and Trustpilot.

- **Repurpose your existing content over several platforms:** Sometimes, your content may not reach everyone in your audience the first time around. Without creating new content, you can repurpose the existing content on different platforms to reach a larger audience and increase your affiliate sales. Let's see how to do it. Imagine your existing content is in a blog post. Based on that, you can create a YouTube video. Then, cut that video into chunks and make a miniseries for Instagram Video (formerly IGTV). Next, you may create an ebook using multiple blog posts.

- **Add new merchants to existing content:** This is another useful strategy to maximize the usage of your old content. Old content is the source of organic search traffic. Therefore, you may refresh the content and add new merchants to your content. Keep in mind to fix broken affiliate links and include up-to-date statistics. Apart from that, you can add CTAs to your long-form articles (articles that are typically 2,000 words or longer). This technique increases your conversion rates. The best practice is to include CTAs at the bottom of the page. Even so, depending on the length, you may include one near the beginning and a few in the middle.

- **Cloak your affiliate links:** Some affiliate links are scary-looking, and users get confused, especially the ones who don't have technical knowledge; for example:

www.sale.com/b=28423gvc=22649urlink=&afftrack =

The majority of users are hesitant to click these kinds of links since they believe it has a virus or some other nefarious purpose. Hence, it's better to cloak your affiliate links to shorten them and to provide information on where the user will end up once they clicked on it.

In comparison to the previous example, the *yoursite.com/go/travelglobe* link is clear and concise. Therefore, this technique increases the likelihood that a user will click on your affiliate link without any hesitation.

In addition to the above-mentioned main strategies, leverage your social media accounts and increase your presence. Similarly, work on and improve your SEO. As I indicated in earlier sections, take maximum advantage of the merchant's marketing resources, such as website banners, logos, sell sheets, usage guidelines, and email templates.

Commission payouts have different structures and timelines depending on the affiliate program terms. Here are the various ways that affiliate marketers get paid:

- **Pay-per-sale:** Here, affiliate marketers get a percentage of the sale price of the product or service for every sale they generated. This is the most common payout structure in affiliate marketing.

- **Pay-per-lead:** Affiliate marketers get paid for every lead they generate. A lead could be subscribing to a newsletter, an online form submission, trial creation, downloading files, any pre-purchase, and many more.

- **Pay-per-click:** The affiliate marketer gets paid for every click that was generated, regardless of whether a lead or sale happened. This is fairly rare in affiliate marketing since all the risk is on the product creator.

Usually, payments were related monthly but this may vary according to the affiliate program terms and conditions. Therefore, before you register with an affiliate program, ensure to check the detailed regard to payments.

It's now your turn to determine how to drive traffic to your affiliate sites, how to get clicks for the affiliate links, and how to convert clicks to sales based on the knowledge you obtained through Steps 7–10. To begin, list some activities to enhance the effectiveness of your affiliate campaigns and boost affiliate sales.

Chapter 5:

The Top Strategies and Tools of Affiliate Marketing

CEO of Flynndustries LLC, Pat Flynn, once mentioned: "Affiliate marketing is not a 'push-button' solution. It takes focus and commitment, and a certain choreography to make it happen the way you want it to" (Convertful, 2019). As he emphasized, you have to identify the best affiliate marketing strategies and tools that work for you while working hard. Therefore, this chapter covers some of these comprehensively.

Create a Website

One of your primary goals on the road to becoming a successful affiliate marketer is to build trust with your audience. If your audience trusts your content, you'll be rewarded with a loyal following. Creating quality content that you have absolute control over is fundamental to establishing your reputation and gaining your audience's trust.

Having your own website is the ideal starting point. Not only does it mean you have complete autonomy over your content, but it can also play a central role in other marketing tools or platforms that you decide to utilize.

Choose a Domain Name and Web Host

In this step, we look into the technical side of the website. It's better to choose a web host which gives you online server space to store your data, making it accessible for internet users. Also, many web hosts offer domain name registration too. When selecting a web host, ensure you look into the following factors.

Check whether the host provides a stable and fast server speed that helps your website to load smoothly. Then, check their security features, for example, SSL certificates, essential security measures, and regular backups.

Once you have decided on the name of your website, you'll choose a web host. This is where things can get technical, but having an idea of how you want your website to perform will help determine your criteria for selecting a web host. Here are some factors to consider if you're starting out and looking for reliability and affordability. Check that the web host provides a stable and fast server speed.

When it comes to pricing plans, read the small print and understand exactly how much you'll be paying and how often.

Select a Platform to Create Your Website

WordPress is probably the most popular website builder, and it's free! Many web hosts also have a one-click WordPress installer. You don't need to have any knowledge or understanding of coding or HTML. Step-by-step tutorials walk you through how it works.

Customize Your Website

A visually attractive website gives a good first impression to your users and keeps them engaged. First, choose a theme for your website and then install it. After that, customize it using the default theme customizer or a page builder like SeedProd. Next, personalize menus and widgets—which include a list of links to essential pages on your website. Home, blog, shop, and contact, are the typical menu items on a website.

In particular, you can install essential plugins to improve the website's functionality without coding. For example, the Wordfence plugin protects your website from malware, spam, and brute-force attacks. Smush is another important plugin that you can use to compromise images and display high-resolution images without slowing down the website. Additionally, you can incorporate affiliate marketing plugins. For instance, the ThirstyAffiliates plugin will optimize affiliate linking, and the Otter Blocks plugin will display your affiliate links more engagingly.

Create Quality Content

Well-written, high-quality content drives traffic and leads to your website. Also, it keeps engaging and retaining readers. For more details about content writing, you may refer to Step 6 in Chapter 3. Then, prepare a list of content ideas that answer their questions. Surfer SEO is a great tool to generate article ideas. The Content Planner is another useful tool to have an idea of the high-performing articles and queries from the main keyword.

Also, it categorizes queries based on the search intent. To stay consistent, plan and organize your content beforehand. You may use Google Calendar and have specific time frames for writing, editing, and publishing content. To organize the content, you can incorporate project management tools like Asana or Trello's

Editorial Calendar is another useful plugin that you can use to plan content creation from the dashboard.

Then, arrange the content around the best-selling affiliate products or services. Do not forget to monitor the major events in your niche and update the content accordingly. Make use of the headings, subheadings, and bulleted points to create well-structured content. Be mindful about paragraphing and have more white space on your page. As mentioned earlier, anchor text is the clickable text in a hyperlink—use it correctly.

The best practice is to mention precise, descriptive, and short terms which are relevant to the content instead of phrases like *Click here* or *Read more*. Integrate visual elements to break up the text, transmit messages faster than text, and highlight important points. For best results, try to upload content about three to four times a week.

Increase Your Site's Search Engine Visibility

Here are a few tips to create an SEO-friendly affiliate website that ranks higher on search engines. Internal links can be used to link one page to another on your website. Nevertheless, make sure to place them in your homepage content naturally and indicate a clear anchor text. Do the same for your other webpages—be purposeful and don't just place links with no context.

A well-developed internal linking strategy improves SEO ranking and gives a clear direction to the search engines about the website structure. At the end of the page, you may indicate the article recommendations to encourage readers to read them. A guest post is another useful technique that you can use to generate traffic, establish authority, and expand your audience.

A guest post is a content piece that you write for another site. Crucially, the guest posts create backlinks to your own site. To write a guest post, first, you need the approval of the owner of the website. Once they accept it, you can write your content while following the guest-post guidelines.

Likewise, you can use alt text (aka alt descriptions or alt tags). It's an alternative text that describes images, tables, and charts when these elements fail to render after a page loads. Alt text also helps to increase your website accessibility to visitors with disabilities or limitations. The better your accessibility, the higher your site will rank. Therefore, make sure to use descriptive, relevant, and concise alt text.

You can optimize your images by selecting the proper format and compressing them with a free tool like ShortPixel or a plugin like Smush. Keep in mind to check the website speed regularly and identify which aspects you need to fix immediately. You may use a speed tester like Pingdom Tools. Notably, incorporate

Google's Mobile-Friendly Test to identify the mobile-friendliness of the website.

Create and Display Necessary Documentation

Many people don't look into the documentation factor when they create a website. Nonetheless, to build a legal and transparent affiliate marketing business, ensure to prepare the following documents:

- **Affiliate marketing agreement:** This is the contact between an affiliate marketer and the brand. Ideally, this has to be signed by the affiliate marketer before they register for an affiliate program. This document indicates the contract period, commission rates, payout process, and other important terms and conditions.

- **Affiliate marketing disclosure:** This is the statement that you disclose the relationship with the merchant you have. It also informs the visitors of your website about receiving commissions if they purchase the product using the link.

- **Privacy policy:** This document explains how you collect and use visitors' information.

- **Copyright notice:** This section highlights how visitors can use content and graphics on your website. This helps you to protect your content from any theft or fraud.

- **Terms of use and disclaimer:** This document limits your responsibilities for website users' (visitors and contributors) actions. Imagine you let contributors publish content on your website. There, you can mention that those views are not yours but only contributors' opinions.

Once you build your own affiliate marketing website, make sure to promote it on other platforms such as social media and email to grow your audience and increase sales.

Start Blogging

Before moving forward, let's understand what exactly an affiliate blog is. An affiliate blog is a blog that includes affiliate links and is published on the blog section of a website. A blog post can be an article, news piece, story, or guide which covers a specific topic or query. In general, blog posts are educational, and usually contain 600 to more than 2,000 words and other media like images, charts, videos, and infographics.

If you have created your own website, then your blog should be a natural integration of your overall site, consistent in branding, look and feel, and easily accessible from the main navigation bar.

If you have decided to not have a website, but rather a standalone blog, I wouldn't recommend that. However, the process is essentially the same as creating a website: Choose your niche, your blog name, and host provider, then customize and install plugins to enhance overall functionality.

After that, name your blog and have an easy-to-say-and-spell blog name. Try and find an alternative name or two, in case the one you've chosen is already in use on the blog platform. It's a good idea to reflect your brand message through the blog name. Next, activate your blog domain on your chosen blogging platform. WordPress, Blogger, and Wix are the most popular blogging platforms. You need to make sure you manage your blog using a content management system (CMS).

A user-friendly interface, customization, price, extensions, support, marketing capabilities, and security are the key factors you need to consider when choosing a CMS. Additionally, install a beautiful theme and essential plugins to maximize your blog's success.

Yoast is a great plugin that you can use to optimize your titles and meta descriptions to improve search engine visibility. WP Rocket makes your site load a lot faster and boosts your SEO substantially, whereas

Shield Security protects your blog from malicious attackers and blocks spam comments.

This is the time to decide on the cornerstone pages of your blog. Basically, you should include a homepage that tells your visitors what your blog is all about. Then, you may include an *About* page that defines who you are, why you started your blog, and what your vision and mission are. Don't be generic. It's better to go in-depth and connect your life story to the About page.

The *Contact* page is another important page that includes a form for people to contact you and link to your other social media platforms. Now, let's discuss how to write your first blog post.

Again, have a comprehensive understanding of your audience and buyer personas. Brainstorm topics and investigate what's missing from the existing discourse. Most importantly, choose a topic you're passionate and knowledgeable about. Then, identify keywords and analyze your audience's search intent. It's good to take a look at the questions and terms related to that topic. Generate a few different titles and come up with a working title. Next, choose the most suitable blog post type from the below list:

- the list-based post

- the "How to" post

- the "What is" post

- the pillar page post ("Ultimate guide")

- the infographic post

- the *newsjacking* post

After that, prepare a rough outline and create keyword-rich headings (H2) and subheadings (H3). Headings help you to arrange your ideas in a more structured manner. This method helps readers easily pick the articles they need. It also allows Google crawlers to index and rank your content effortlessly.

Once everything is in place, you can start writing the blog post. To grab the reader's attention, first write a captivating introduction. Then, according to the outline you prepared earlier, build out each section and expand on all points as needed. You can add images and other media elements to make your content more visually appealing and useful, but make sure to use them with a purpose.

The best practice is to center your images and keep your sentences clear and concise. To convert your anonymous blog visitors into leads, you have to create a conversion path. For that, add CTAs and alt text to include affiliate links in your blog post.

If you have multiple blog articles, then link to them within your content. You can check Step 6 in Chapter 3 for more details on content writing. Proofread your content and go through a thorough editing process to develop top-notch content. Once you prepare optimized content, you can publish it in your CMS immediately, or save it under drafts for a future scheduled date. Next, promote the blog post across all your available and relevant marketing channels and track its performance regularly.

Create Email Lists

Affiliate email marketing is a method of sharing affiliate links in highly targeted and well-crafted emails. Why do we use emails for affiliate marketing? Is it an effective method? A survey carried out in the US shows 99% of consumers check their email every day, and half of the respondents check their inbox at least 10 times a day (Csizmadia, 2021).

The buying decisions of 59% of consumers were influenced by emails, and 2 out of 3 marketers agree that email represents their biggest return on investment (ROI). Did you know, as of 2023, there are more than 4 billion active email users in the world? (Oberlo, 2023).

As you see, there is huge potential to grow your affiliate marketing through email campaigns. However, before you can launch an email campaign, you must first have an email list. When creating your website, I strongly recommend that you include a data capture form that will automatically collect the email addresses of visitors to your site. However, don't add affiliate links for the sake of it, but rather seamlessly insert them into quality email content.

To launch a successful email campaign, follow these three fundamental steps. First, check if your email provider allows affiliate links because some platforms prevent or restrict the use of affiliate links due to deliverability issues. Secondly, choose the right, relevant, and profitable affiliate links to promote. Finally, add affiliate links to your email sequences and track the performance of your email campaign.

Let's dive into some affiliate email marketing best practices. First, segment your email list based on smaller targeted consumer groups, preferences, and behavior. Accordingly, share the most relevant information with the email users. Trigger emails are delivered to your audience depending on the preset events, conditions, or users' behavior.

Segment- and event-based are the main two types of trigger emails. Segment-based emails can be shared when your subscribers meet certain conditions, whereas event-based emails can be shared when your subscribers opt-in or make a purchase.

Additionally, it's always best to share more personalized emails whenever you can, to position yourself as an authority in your niche and build a closer relationship with your audience. Moreover, optimize your email content to attract your audience to what you're promoting.

Always personalize your email communications. Make sure your data capture form, in addition to collecting email addresses, also collects first names—at a minimum.

Why Is an Affiliate Marketing Email List Important?

As we discussed above, email marketing is one of the most cost-effective methods that can be used in affiliate marketing, and it provides a specific, well-tailored pitch to contact your target audience. In this section, we discuss how to build an email list and its importance for your affiliate marketing. An email list is a collection of emails that you gathered from people who have signed up to receive emails from individuals or organizations.

Why do you need an email list? There is no way to contact your users again unless you've got their contact details. This is the main reason you need to create an email list, and it allows you to create personalized communication with your audience. It builds a loyal customer base and increases their trust. A precise email list helps you to easily reach numerous customers and facilitates delivering product updates or providing special discounts, coupons, or deals. Here's how you can create an affiliate marketing email list.

- **Sign up for an email provider:** Before signing up for an email provider, check whether they allow you to conduct affiliate marketing and, accordingly, get their permission first. There are two types of permissions you may need to send emails to your audience: Implied permission means you already have a relationship with your receiver, whereas express permission means you don't have any existing relationship with the receiver, and they need to express their permission before you're allowed to send them emails.

In general, you'll most likely encounter the need for express permission when creating an email list. ConvertKit, GetResponse, Mailchimp, AWeber, Brevo (formerly Sendinblue), and Drip are providers that typically allow affiliate marketing links, and they offer good support as well.

- **Use a conversion optimization toolkit:** To grab users' attention, you can use conversion optimization features in your email content. Floating bars, gamified wheels, lightbox pop-ups, scroll boxes, page-level targeting, geolocation targeting, exit intention detection, and other templates are the most effective conversion optimization features. OptinMonster is a great tool for this, and it provides analytical tools like A/B testing to analyze the performance of email marketing campaigns.

- **Optimize your site with sign-up forms and offer lead magnets:** If you ask for too many steps to complete in a sign-up form, users might not fill it out. Therefore, it's highly important to make it easy for them to do so. WPForms is a great form-building tool. Bear in mind, you need to check whether your sign-up form is visible to your audience. It is best to try out different timings for pop-ups to test what works for you.

Why would users give you their contact details and sign up? What will they get for this transaction in return? This way, you have to offer a lead magnet immediately to make your users happy and make them feel they are valued. This is like you placing some icing on your deal. Product samples, content roundups, quizzes, training videos, ebooks, giveaways, free guides, consultations, and templates are the most effective lead magnets.

- **Create automated emails:** A steady stream of emails is crucial to keeping your audience engaged. Hence, an automated and prepared email flow will make it easy for you. This technique saves you time and assures you send out the right emails at the right moment.

- **Produce great content:** Content is one of your most powerful marketing tools, don't hesitate to invest in it. Therefore, your content needs to be informative, valuable, entertaining, and unique for subscribers to keep reading your emails. Always try to deliver what your subscribers might like to read or might enjoy instead of what you want them to read.

Nevertheless, creating personalized email content frequently is not an easy task. However, thanks to artificial intelligence, you can rely on automation tools. HubSpot's Campaign Assistant is a great tool to customize your emails.

Your first or welcome email is the most important to create a good impression on your subscribers. Use your welcome email to set expectations and tell what you deliver and how frequently you'll be in contact. Always value and respect the reader's time. Therefore, make sure to keep your emails precise and simple.

Additionally, don't try to push affiliate links in every content you share with your subscribers. So, it's best to add your affiliate offers to the emails organically. Furthermore, it's best to include other peoples' opinions to add social proof to your content. Remember to personally follow up on your subscribers and avoid using the auto-responder feature. This way, your responses sound more personal, which helps with retaining your audience.

To save time, you can turn your most successful and productive emails into templates. Then, you can use them over and over while adding some small personal touches. Be mindful of the fact that being consistent will make your audience remember you.

- **Expand your audience:** To lengthen your email list, add social sharing buttons and an "email to a friend" button to ensure your subscribers can forward your emails to their friends, colleagues, and so on. Be sure to include a "Subscribe" CTA button in the emails so that new people who receive your emails can also subscribe to you.

- **Segment your affiliate marketing email list:** It's not possible to write individual emails for each subscriber in your email list. Still, segmentation by buyer personas helps you to offer a high level of personalization. Highly targeted emails increase your CTRs and increase the chances of affiliate sales.

Now, let's briefly discuss how to grow your email list using various social media platforms.

- **Facebook:** You can publish something special about your email newsletter in your Facebook profile cover photo. You can then publish the snippets and highlights of your email newsletter as a post. It entices your followers to sign up for your newsletter. In addition, place a sign-up email newsletter CTA button somewhere in that post or within your profile. Similarly, you can use those posts to encourage email submission to access more details.

- **YouTube:** To generate further engagement from your YouTube viewers, you can use your end screens also known as video outros to add hyperlinks to your email sign-up landing page. Also, you can place your sign-up page link in your channel header and video descriptions.

- **Instagram:** You may use your Instagram bio and posts to place an email sign-up CTA. In particular, you can use the swipe-up feature to share your landing page and add an email button to your business profile.

- **LinkedIn:** Similar to other social media platforms, you can post highlights about the email newspaper content on LinkedIn with an email sign-up CTA. Another possibility is sharing links to your sign-up pages through conversations.

In addition to social media platforms, your website is one of the great resources to strengthen your email list. Likewise, you can make use of the traditional marketing methods. You can collect email addresses from attendees at trade shows, seminars, educational panels, meetups, hackathons, conferences, online webinars, and networking events.

Use Influencer Marketing

Most people think affiliate and influencer marketing are the same. Yet, there are key differences—thus, let's identify them first. As you already know, in affiliate marketing, you're only paid a commission for making a lead toward a merchant's website, and it's mainly based on conversion rates. Nevertheless, affiliate marketers don't get paid for increased web traffic or brand awareness.

On the other hand, in influencer marketing, you're paid for increased traffic, improved brand awareness, and driven messages to brands' target audiences. Influencers usually have a larger social following with authentic, credible, and sustainable inbound traffic, plus, they have different compensation types such as commission, flat rate fees, product gifting, or a combination of all three.

However, in practice, influencer marketing results can't be guaranteed since many influencers have many fake followers. Hence, a combination of affiliate and influencer marketing can still be better. In the past, we usually depend on our family or friends' recommendations or other consumer reviews. Nowadays, many Gen Zs rely on influencer recommendations, and it shows that influencer recommendations are much more powerful than ever before.

Moreover, influencer marketing influences purchases through authentic content, improves brand awareness, plus establishes social proof. In summary, influencer marketing has a high ROI, and it saves you money plus time. Let's identify the various types of influencers below.

- **Nano-, micro-, and macro-influencers:** Nano-influencers usually have 1–10,000 followers, whereas micro-influencers have between 50,000 and 100,000 followers. Macro-influencers generally have more than 100,000 followers, and they often don't focus on one niche. They create content through social media platforms, blogs, forums, websites, and so on.

- **Celebrity influencers:** Generally, celebrity influencers are the ones who are famous and have millions of followers. They are very good at influencing because they are widely recognized in many industries.

- **Blog influencers:** These types of influencers have well-established blogs with thousands or millions of subscribers and readers.

- **Social media influencers:** They are well-recognized on social media platforms and have thousands or even millions of followers. Normally, they cover a wide range of topics through their content.

- **Key opinion leaders:** These are trusted influencers and are experts on a specialized topic within a particular field.

Once you identify the right type of influencers you're required to work with, it's time to reach out to them. However, the question is: How do you find them? What platforms do you need to use? I'll back you up. One of the most straightforward ways to find influencers is through Google or any search engine. You can simply type in the industry-related terms and keywords into the search bar to locate the specific articles or posts that link you to influencers' contact details.

Alternatively, you may search on industry-specific sites and webpages. Social media platforms are another great way to reach influencers. You may use particular keywords or phrases, hashtags, competitors' social media accounts, and tagged posts to locate the right ones.

Bear in mind that you should check the comment section in influencers' social media posts to determine whether they interacted with their followers effectively. Reading blogs is another significant way to locate influencers and understand the quality of their work.

In particular, you may use software like BuzzSumo, BuzzStream, and Modash to identify influencers and measure their success. Alternatively, when you're looking for a celebrity influencer, the above-mentioned methods and dropping an email or giving a call will definitely not work. Therefore, it's best to reach them via a talent agency or an agent.

As of now, you have an idea of the sources you need to use to locate influencers. The next step is to approach them. Nonetheless, simply dropping a message saying, "I want to work with you," won't take you far. Here is a list of steps you need to follow to successfully partner with influencers and create a seamless influencer marketing strategy to support your affiliate marketing process. You may consider this section as a summary of this heading as well.

- **Study the market:** As a first step, investigate the market and learn what your competitors do in your niche and what they sell. Analyze the popularity of their affiliate programs and identify what techniques they use to attract affiliate marketers or influencers.

- **Determine your campaign goals:** Decide whether you try to increase brand awareness or drive engagement. If you want to generate leads, likewise, have a clear understanding of the outcome of your affiliate and influencer marketing strategy. Based on that, set SMART (specific, measurable, achievable, relevant, and time-bound) goals and objectives.

- **Define your campaign audience:** Regardless of which type of influencer you work with or the different ways they use to connect with their followers, your target audience, buyer personas, and your marketing goals remain the same. Therefore, first, identify your potential audience and their desires.

- **Set your budget and choose your influencer type:** The next step is to take care of the numbers. This is the factor that most affiliate marketers or influencers look for before they partner with you. Decide how much you're going to pay for them according to your budget. If you're a startup, you may opt to use a nano-influencer, whereas if you're a huge company, you may think of partnering with a macro or celebrity influencer. Accordingly, it's best to determine what type of influencer and content is aligned with your audience.

- **Shortlist influencers:** Once you identify the type of influencer, it's time to spread the word to hire the right influencer. You may post an ad, or you may use the contacting methods we discussed earlier to locate and choose the right fit for your business. When considering an influencer's eligibility, you may ask yourself the below questions to make a better decision:

  o Do these influencers and their lifestyles fit my brand and its image?

  o Does this person have a personality I want to work with?

- o Who is this influencer's current audience?

- o Does working with this influencer make sense for my budget?

- o Have they worked with any of my competitors?

- o Is my target audience active on the platform primarily used by this influencer?

- o Has this influencer actually used any of my products or services before? Are they a customer?

- o What will this influencer expect from me?

Additionally, ensure to review their work and measure the success.

- **Outreach messaging:** Once you have chosen a specific influencer, it's time to contact them. To grab influencers' attention, it's best if you can customize your message by indicating the following areas: First, introduce yourself and your company.; then, mention how you found the influencer; and third, offer your affiliate partnership.

- **Finalize campaign expectations with your influencer:** This is the most important step of the process. Once the influencer agrees to partner with you, you have to be very clear with what you have for them, as well as any expectations they have for you. Make sure to submit these expectations in written format, agreed upon, and signed by both parties. Some of the common expectations to review:

o   How will influencers join your affiliate program?

o   How long has your partnership been valid?

o   How will influencers be paid or rewarded (commission, money, discounts, coupon codes, swag [for example, clothing, accessories, or product samples], free products or services, etc.)?

o   How will you be communicating with the influencer?

o   Are any other terms or conditions of the contract necessary to review?

Once you finalize the deal with the influencer, they will start working according to the predetermined campaign goals. Keep in mind, you need to measure the results of the campaigns based on different KPIs such as engagement, reach, resonance, conversions (the number of leads), clicks, brand awareness, ROI, and follower count. KPIs depend on your campaign goals and requirements.

For instance, if you wish to achieve only affiliate marketing results through the campaign, then you may have to look into the conversion rates, whereas if you wish to achieve both influencer and affiliate marketing results, then you may have to rely on each KPI mentioned above.

Get a Microsite

Microsites are niche and mini-websites that are separate from a main website and designed to promote products for targeted, specific audiences. A microsite structure varies from single pages to a collection of them, and it may have its own domain or is a sub-domain of the main site. Both brands and affiliate marketers create microsites to promote products, individual events, campaigns, and content.

To be successful with microsites, make sure to write detailed, media-rich content, highlight the features of products and services to grab viewers' attention, and add reviews to build trust. Moreover, you may use a combination of products from different affiliate programs and have a range of products at various price points.

Maximize Social Media

As I emphasized throughout this book, social media is one of the greatest platforms for affiliate marketing for many reasons. Specifically, for beginners, social media is a good option because it's free to use. When social media users promote your products and services, it provides a better impression of your brand, increases the brand's social media presence, and helps you to get more customers. Since there are various social media platforms, you can select whichever ones fit your brand:

- **Facebook:** A Facebook profile, page, and groups are the three options that you can use mainly to promote affiliate links.

- **YouTube:** As of 2023, YouTube has over 2.68 billion active monthly users of all age groups (Ruby, 2022). Video marketing is a highly beneficial method, and you may use your channel to post how-to videos, product reviews, guides, unboxing videos, and more. It's better to indicate the affiliate link in the video or put it in the description box to send viewers directly to your affiliate products and services.

- **Instagram:** You may promote your affiliate links through regular posts, reels, stories, Instagram Video, highlights, swipe-up features, Instagram Shops, and the link-in-bio option.

- **TikTok:** TikTok is the most trending social media platform at the moment. You can go viral with your content within just a few seconds if you publish creative and unique short videos.

- **Pinterest:** This is popular image-based content and is most known for providing ideas and inspiration. You may post product reviews and descriptions, infographics, and promotional materials, and create product collections plus checklists on Pinterest.

- **Twitter (aka X):** This is a great platform to establish yourself as a reliable and trustworthy source of information, as well as present yourself as an expert in your niche. It's a good idea to add a human touch to affiliate promotions while using humorous content and headlines. Make sure to post frequently and use trending hashtags to reach new customers, followers, and leads quickly.

In reality, not all of these platforms will reach your target audience and generate the clicks you want. Therefore, it's essential to pick the right social media platform for your affiliate marketing strategy. There are a few steps that will help you with that decision. To become successful in affiliate marketing, you must go to the consumers instead of waiting for them to find you.

Identify which platform your potential customers are available mostly. As of 2023, Facebook is the leading social media platform (Iskiev, 2023). YouTube takes second place and Instagram is third. Subsequently, analyze your competitors and check where they are promoting their products and services. Analyze the feedback and engagement on different platforms of competitors, and identify what you can do differently than them.

I don't personally recommend trying each platform because it's a waste of time and effort. What you can simply do is narrow down each platform's pros, cons, features, and so on. Then, cross-check them with your products and their capabilities. For example, if you wish to post a detailed description of the products, Twitter isn't a good option, since it will limit your posts to 280 characters—unless you have a Twitter Blue subscription which allows up to 4,000 characters.

Most importantly, come up with a powerful content strategy. Decide what kind of content you plan to post and how often. For instance, generally, it's better to post three YouTube videos per week, whereas for TikTok videos it's one to four times a day.

Next, evaluate what you're good at, and analyze whether you have skills in making videos, images, reels, blog posts, and so on. For example, if you're not capable of making videos, choosing YouTube or TikTok as your main social media streams is an utter loss. To create click-worthy content, use social media platforms' features and tools effectively. Likewise, analyze all these areas and choose the most suitable social media platform for your affiliate marketing process. Once you select particular platforms, you can use them for better and higher results.

As soon as your affiliate program is up and running, make sure you continuously optimize it. It's better to update product or service information, sales, and promotions details regularly. Moreover, you can create vanity coupon codes and run viral giveaways to get followers' attention easily. Alternatively, you can convert your website visitors into social media followers by embedding social media feeds to your website.

Smash Balloon is a collection of social media feed plugins that can be used in this task, and it's workable on Facebook, Instagram, and Twitter. It's another good way to connect with social media influencers, and you may use affiliate networks such as BuzzSumo, FlexOffers, Awin, and ShareASale to find them. Adding social media widgets to your website is another great technique to use, since it allows your visitors to share your site's content to their social profiles. Here also, you can use Smash Balloon as a tool.

I believe now you're clear on how to use social media platforms as a supportive tool for your affiliate marketing. Based on the information we discussed in this chapter as well as according to your business goals, it's now time to determine the most effective marketing strategy for your affiliate marketing business; whether it's a website, blog, email marketing, influencer marketing, microsites, or social media platforms. Once you're confident with your choice, take the necessary steps to implement it.

In Chapter 6, we identified the top strategies in affiliate marketing. Building a website can be considered a foundation for affiliate marketing, and it's important to build trust and authority in the entire marketing process. Choosing a niche and deciding on a website type are the first few steps to creating a website.

Subsequently, you have to choose a domain name, web host, and platform. Next, develop a customized website and quality content using various tools, as discussed, to attract more users. Keep in mind that you need to check whether your website is visible to search engines. Likewise, you may create your own blog and publish it as a webpage on your website.

Email lists are useful to grab the attention of the users who frequently check emails for your affiliate marketing campaign. Alternatively, you may conduct a combination of affiliate and influencer marketing to maximize the results of your campaign. Based on your campaign goals, choose an influencer to partner with.

Nano or micro are the most feasible options for a beginner. With time, you may think of partnering with even a macro or celebrity influencer. Microsites and social media platforms are other suitable platforms to run your affiliate marketing campaigns.

Nonetheless, it isn't necessary to stick to one particular platform or method. You may cross-promote the different content among various platforms. For example, you can publish a Facebook post about your email newsletter or blog. Still, it's best to identify the most feasible options according to your campaign goals, target audience, as well as capabilities.

When you narrow down your affiliate marketing into certain platforms or methods, it helps you to provide more customized and rich content for your audience. On the other hand, it saves you money, time, and effort. In the next chapter, we discuss the best affiliate marketing programs and networks.

Chapter 6:

Best Affiliate Marketing

Programs and Networks

So far, we've discussed affiliate programs and networks multiple times. What are the most popular options available in the market? What are their features and usages? This chapter will cover these areas in depth and introduce the best programs and networks for affiliate marketing. At the end of the chapter, we discuss some real examples of affiliate marketing, especially targeting first-time affiliate marketers. Let's start with affiliate programs.

Best Affiliate Marketing Programs

Finding the best affiliate program is one of the biggest challenges most affiliate marketers face. However, choosing the wrong affiliate program could be the biggest mistake you make. Therefore, having an in-depth understanding of affiliate programs is essential to becoming successful in affiliate marketing. As promised in Chapter 3, here are some of the more popular affiliate programs for your consideration. We start with ecommerce businesses, then marketers.

Best Affiliate Programs for Ecommerce Businesses

- **Amazon Associates:** This is one of the oldest affiliate programs out there, and is a great affiliate program if you're a novice to affiliate marketing. Amazon's brand name, extensive product range, easy-to-use affiliate dashboards, and high conversion rates are some of the key advantages of this program. However, you need to have a Facebook, Instagram, YouTube, or Twitter account to qualify. Amazon will review the number of followers you have, together with other engagement metrics in your social media accounts, to ascertain if you're eligible for the program.

  In March 2017, Amazon launched its Influencer Program as an extension to the Associates program while specifically targeting social media influencers. The commission usually varies from 1% to 20%, depending on the product category. The cookie is valid for only 24 hours, and direct deposit, check, or an Amazon gift card are the payment methods.

- **Shopify:** This is a complete platform that allows users to start, grow, and manage a business. Merchants can build their own online stores and sell their products in different places and platforms. When it comes to affiliate marketers, they can benefit from the Shopify affiliate program. This program is free to join and is best for course instructors, influencers, bloggers, and video marketers. There are thousands of global course educators, content creators, review sites, and influencers included in the Shopify affiliate program.

Affiliate marketers can earn a competitive referral commission, and have access to multiple educational materials to support content creation and conversion rates. Commission rates vary depending on the merchant, and the cookie duration is a healthy 30 days. There should be a minimum balance of $10 before withdrawals, and direct bank deposits and PayPal are the payment methods.

- **Rakuten:** This is a Japanese affiliate marketing service provider and one of the oldest affiliate networks. It acquired LinkShare in 2005. Rakuten's affiliate program connects over 2,500 different retailers that sell a wide range of products, and they offer three types of commission rates (dynamic commissioning, coupon commissioning, and multitouch commissioning). However, the commission rates and the cookie lifespan depend on the merchant. They distribute the payment as a direct deposit or check.

- **eBay Partner Network:** A diverse selection of products and a globally recognized brand name with high conversion rates are the advantages of eBay's affiliate program. Commission rates range from 1% to 4% but mainly depend on the product category. Cookie duration is valid only for 24 hours. Direct deposit and PayPal are the payment methods.

Best Affiliate Programs for Marketers

- **Semrush:** Semrush is a leading SEO tool that provides multiple services such as keyword research and rank tracking. The Semrush Affiliate Program is best suited for affiliate marketers, course creators, agencies, and paid search specialists. Commission rates vary depending on the referral type. The cookie duration is 120 days.

- **Leadpages:** Leadpages is a popular landing page and website builder. Its affiliate program offers from 10% to 50% recurring commissions for every sale and is open to everyone. The cookie's lifespan is 90 days. PayPal or Stripe are the payment methods.

- **HubSpot:** This is a well-known customer relationship management platform that offers content management, sales, marketing, and customer service all in one place. The HubSpot Affiliate Program is best suited to content creators, bloggers, and so forth. It's free to join, and HubSpot provides an array of educational resources for its affiliates. There are 3 commission rate tiers, with the 1st tier having a recurring monthly rate of 30% for up to 1 year. Cookie duration is a generous 180 days, and electronic funds transfer or PayPal are the available payment methods.

Here is a list of other affiliate programs suited for marketers.

- ConvertKit

- Fiverr

- Elementor

- Contact

- Bluehost

- Calendly

- Loom

- ClickFunnels

- Teachable

- NordVPN

- Wordable

- AWeber

Best Affiliate Marketing Networks

We briefly covered the affiliate network in Chapter 1. Here, I provide an in-depth overview of affiliate networks. Affiliate networks work as a marketplace for affiliate programs by connecting affiliate marketers to thousands of brands. There are numerous benefits to joining an affiliate network. You can select a wide range of products and services relevant to your audience. Depending on your performance, some affiliate networks offer rewards and incentives.

Typically, you don't need to chase payments because the platform handles them for you. One of the significant advantages of an affiliate network is that you can track your progress easily using analytics and reporting tools. However, some affiliate networks offer very low commission rates, and some of them require you to have a specific amount of traffic to apply.

Here is a list of key factors to consider when choosing an affiliate network. First, review the background information of the company running the network, such as their annual reports. Secondly, examine the affiliate network's starting fees and binding agreement. Avoid paying a starting fee or fixed monthly fee because an affiliate network makes money when it delivers traffic to your site.

If a network requests you to pay such charges, take it as a sign that they don't have the confidence they can deliver enough traffic to you for it to be profitable for them. Also, avoid entering into any agreements that go beyond a 3-month duration.

Thirdly, research where your competitors are active. Rather than avoiding the competition, select a network where your competitors are most active. Fourthly, analyze other brands and businesses connected to the affiliate network. Investigate whether the affiliate network associates with any brands or businesses that don't align with your values. Don't measure the quality of the network based on the number of affiliate marketers. Rather, evaluate based on the quality of work by the affiliate marketers in the network.

Transparency is another critical factor that you must take into account. There are some networks called black box networks—generally, they don't disclose details regarding the origin of web traffic and other important information. It's best to avoid such networks. Next, focus on the techniques that affiliate networks use for tracking and reporting. Crucially, analyze their support and how fast they are at answering your queries. Let's briefly take a look at some of the most famous affiliate networks below.

- **ClickBank:** This is an easy-to-join global affiliate marketing platform and is good for all levels of affiliate marketers. ClickBank provides access to a wide range of physical and digital products such as arts, entertainment, games, business, marketing, languages, and self-help. Commission rates are up to 90%, but the majority are lower. Direct deposit, check, and wire transfer are the main payment methods.

- **ShareASale:** This is a Chicago-based affiliate network and one of the largest players in the affiliate marketing industry. This network connects with over 4,000 programs and includes a wide range of products (art, clothing, accessories, automotive, computers, and even online dating). ShareASale has over 1.2 million registered affiliate marketers and is good for new or established affiliate marketers interested in promoting physical products.

  Global affiliate network, Awin, acquired ShareASale in 2017 to expand its international affiliate opportunities. Commission rates usually average between 5% and 20% but mostly depend on the merchant.

In the previous two sections, we identified various types of affiliate programs and networks. After analyzing their various features, hopefully, you can select the most appropriate one for you. Don't worry if you don't get it the first time. Take what you've learned from the experience and become a more successful affiliate marketer in the long term! Next, we discuss affiliate marketing examples to inspire you on your journey.

Examples of Affiliate Marketing to Inspire Your Own

So far, we've covered everything you need to start your own affiliate marketing campaign. Now, let's take a look at some practical examples to inspire you. Bear in mind, most of these campaigns are run by larger businesses, but you can take the principles used here and apply them in your own affiliate marketing business.

The Barbecue Lab

The Barbecue Lab specializes in outdoor cooking, and it covers small get-togethers to large events. In general, it publishes a combination of a YouTube video and a blog post for the target keyword.

Let's assume the target phrase is, "smokeless fire pit." Its YouTube video title reads, "Which Smokeless Fire Pit Is Best? | Breeo Y-Series vs Solo Stove Bonfire 2.0," and its blog post is titled, "5 Best Smokeless Fire Pits of 2023." Alongside YouTube, it uses Facebook, Instagram, Twitter, and Pinterest accounts. As you see, you also can run your affiliate marketing campaign on different platforms using different techniques.

Simply Insurance

Simply Insurance is an online digital insurance agency. When we analyze its affiliate marketing strategy, guest posts were its secret to success. It managed to write 1,000 guest posts, acquire more backlinks, and collect over 2,200 referring domains in just two years.

Hobotech

Hobotech is a YouTuber who films and publishes videos as reviews and comparisons of expensive (typically costing thousands of dollars) electrical products like solar power stations and lithium batteries. For instance, recently, he published a video about a portable solar power station that received nearly half a million views (Widmer, 2023). The electronic gadget costs over $2,000. Imagine if he receives a minimum 10% commission rate—he has probably earned tens of thousands of dollars.

Nonetheless, he does not use any latest camera gear or fancy editing techniques for his videos. Also, his videos are not overly entertaining. So, what makes his affiliate marketing stand out? He breaks down complex topics into ways that anyone can understand, and he explains everything in-depth. Furthermore, he never recommended any product that isn't actually worth the money. All of these activities help him to stand as a trustworthy source of information, yielding him more subscribers and more profits.

Scotty Kilmer

The owner of the YouTube channel is a mechanic with over 40 years of experience. His YouTube content helps more people work on their vehicles on their own. There are more than 5.5 million YouTube subscribers on his channel (Widmer, 2023). According to his affiliate marketing strategy, he first publishes a video teaching how to do certain tasks on their cars. Then, he links and mentions all the tools and parts needed in the video description. His videos explain everything simply and include high-quality content. That's the main reason behind his success.

Wirecutter

Wirecutter is a product review site and affiliate marketing website that sold over $20 million worth of products in 2018 (Widmer, 2023). There are certain key critical success factors of its affiliate marketing strategy. The first thing is that it provides an excellent user experience with an ad-free, mobile-friendly layout, and has great website navigation and category pages. It frequently updates its content and shares it through email and social media.

As you observed, different businesses use different platforms and techniques. There is no clear-cut way to run an affiliate marketing campaign. Use the knowledge you gained throughout this book and develop your own customized campaign. Yes, you can do it! The next chapter looks at some things you need to put in mind before embarking on your affiliate marketing endeavor.

Chapter 7:

Special Considerations to Remember Before Your Start

In this section, we will discuss a few critical facts that you need to consider before you get started with affiliate marketing. First, I plan to share some tips to become a successful affiliate marketer. Subsequently, we discuss the mistakes that you need to avoid. In the latter part of the section, some key trends in affiliate marketing for your future reference are introduced.

Tips to Help You Become a Successful Affiliate Marketer

You may consider this section as a summary of the important points we discussed earlier. Also, I have included some tips based on my personal experiences as well. So, let's dive into them.

Know How Much Money You Want to Make

In reality, we all do business to make money, am I right? So, it's better to have a monetary goal for your affiliate business, and it's up to you to decide whether you need to make $100, $1,000, or even $100,000 per month. Based on that goal, you can decide how much time, money, and energy you have to invest. For instance, you can decide how often you want to work on your business. Every day? Three times a week or once a week? Or else, do you have to work 24/7?

How much money do you need to allocate as a beginner? Be clear with your goals plus how much work you want to put in. Apart from that, decide whether affiliate marketing will be a core stream of income for your business. In certain situations, money is not the only motivation to do business. So, have a clear understanding of what the main reason or driving force is behind why you want to have a business.

Gain Your Audience's Trust and Increase Engagement

To obtain the best results from affiliate marketing and create repeat visitors, building and maintaining the audience's trust is highly important. Affiliate disclosure is the foremost feature that leads to getting visitors' trust. Also, working with a merchant that provides relevant products or services to your audience and a brand that shares the same values as you are the other crucial factors. Moreover, having a legal and ethical affiliate marketing strategy is another great practice that helps you to build audience trust.

In particular, make sure to prevent any kind of affiliate marketing scammers, which some marketers use to cheat the system for higher income. Cookie dropping also known as stuffing, URL hijacking, click spam (often called click flooding), and fake leads are the main affiliate marketing scammers that you must avoid. To create an engaged community, have conversations with your visitors. How can you do that?

For instance, if you have a blog, allow comments and start dialogues with your readers by replying to their comments. You may include texts like, "Would you like more information on this topic?" or, "Tell us your opinion!" at the end of your blog posts. These CTAs foster community interaction and increase your conversions.

Create Quality and Solid Content

A successful distribution strategy ensures that products or services reach the target market. For affiliate marketing, content marketing is the most suitable answer. So, every time, try your best to create reader-centric, accessible, and engaging content in which you provide detailed information and answer their questions. Knowledge and expertise can distinguish you from your competitors.

Therefore, without marketing the products for the sole purpose of making money, be sure to have an in-depth understanding of the items you promote. In any event, prevent promoting substandard products from suspicious vendors, since it ruins the audience's trust over time. At all times, make it your top priority to promote valuable products or services from credible partners.

When choosing a merchant, another thing you have to look at is whether they have good landing pages. Unpleasant or spammy-looking landing pages confuse your visitors. If a landing page includes low-quality content, an outdated design, superfluous ads, or lots of CTAs—it's best to reconsider the partnership you have with your merchant. Rather than selling, always provide up-to-date quality information that visitors find useful so that they keep coming back.

To stay current with industry trends, you may participate in forum discussions and subscribe to industry-related blogs. Additionally, it's better to stick to one niche and use one particular site for it. If you really want, you may create various sites for different niches. Bonus tip: To help customers make their buying decision quickly, you may include product reviews, tutorials, and comparisons in your content. On the other hand, this technique helps you to boost your affiliate sales as well.

Provide Bonuses and Share Promo Codes

Providing bonuses is another effective way of giving a reason for visitors to click on your affiliate link. Bonuses can be anything that the target market enjoys; for example, free templates, ebooks, software, or support. Promo codes like discounts, coupons, and gift codes increase the chances of your audience buying from your affiliate links, and it attracts new customers.

So, talk to your merchants and see whether they like to provide redeemable promo codes for their products. Once they agree, you can spread the news through your other platforms as well. For example, place an affiliate banner on your website and share it as a social media post.

Particularly, you can use limited-time deals to stimulate visitors to act quickly. However, overusing promo codes might train customers to wait for a better deal. So, be mindful of the timing factor! According to my experience, I usually prefer publishing promo codes during product launches and holidays. Alternatively, peak seasons like Christmas evening and Valentine's Day are the best periods to run ads and increase web traffic; thus, making more money.

Scrutinize the Feasibility of Promoting Digital Products

Digital products like ebooks and software are intangible assets and can be delivered in electronic formats. Therefore, the customer can access the products instantly once they complete a purchase. On the other hand, you don't have to worry about whether the product is in stock.

For merchants, there are no storage, shipping, and duplication costs for digital products. Because of that, they have the freedom to share a higher commission rate with the affiliate marketers who promote them. So, if you're interested in digital products or services, you should consider them.

Improve Your Process

Affiliate marketing is also an ongoing learning process and effort. In other words, ongoing development and continuous commitment are required to be successful. While improving, don't forget to track the process. What pages get the majority of your traffic? What pages are visited most before a conversion? What links on each page get clicked?

Likewise, use your data and analytics to determine what kind of new actions to be implemented. Furthermore, use local SEO practices to reach the local community effectively. Therefore, create localized content using local keywords, register in local business listings, and enroll in local online directories. In addition, keep the NAP (name, address, and phone number) citation uniform across different channels to improve an affiliate website's local rankings.

Affiliate Marketing Mistakes to Avoid

I have highlighted the mistakes you should avoid in many sections. Let's briefly discuss them again. Choosing the wrong niche or working in an uninteresting niche is the most common mistake that many affiliate marketers make. So, go for an interesting niche that is commonly researched by consumers.

Not having a sufficient or deep understanding of what you're promoting is another common fault. This is the main reason: You have to select a niche that you're knowledgeable about. Promoting a product or service that doesn't make sense for your target audience or promoting too many products are other mistakes you must avoid.

Pat Flynn once said, "Many people who get into affiliate marketing do so with the same mindset: making money first, and thinking of their audience second (if they think of them at all!). That's a recipe for disaster—or at least lousy results" (Convertful, 2019).

As he mentioned, if you prioritize selling over helping or choosing quantity over quality, that creates a negative impact on your affiliate marketing campaign. Similarly, if you focus on product or service features in your content instead of benefits, it won't be useful for your audience's experience. At the same time, publishing low-quality content with a lack of evergreen content is another blunder. Therefore, always be honest with what you promote and do your best for your target audience.

I have observed that some affiliate marketers have unrealistic income goals. As a result, they always tend to select the most expensive products to promote without having proper experience or interest in them. Nevertheless, I don't recommend that strategy to anyone because the chances of failing are high.

Going overboard with promotions and copying others' work are other faults that you must omit at any cost. Apart from that, don't expect visitors to your platforms without making any effort. So, consistent hard work is a key factor to becoming successful in affiliate marketing.

Many affiliate marketers misinterpret that they should analyze their affiliate marketing campaign performance, SEO, and site speed at the beginning only. Yet, it's a process that you must continue throughout your journey. With all this in mind, I'm sure by now you understand the areas that you must prevent or avoid beforehand.

Even so, imagine you made a mistake. Nothing to worry about, everyone makes mistakes, but a mistake is not a factor to give up. So, learn from the mistake and continue your process. The most important thing you have to do is to not make the same mistake twice!

Future Trends in Affiliate Marketing

The affiliate marketing industry is constantly evolving and growing. Therefore, you must monitor all the trends in affiliate marketing including the industries, products, platforms, and channels to identify the possible opportunities arising in the field. Here is a list of top affiliate marketing trends to keep an eye on.

- **Influencer marketing:** More influencer partnerships can be seen among affiliate marketers, and many of them have chosen nano- and micro-influencers. The main reason for that is, nano- and micro-influencers fall under the micro-niche bubble. Due to that, their popularity among their followers is much greater than macro-influencers.

  So, their brand recognition, authority, trust, engagement, and loyalty to your product or service are high. Compared to macro-influencers, micro- or nano-influencers are cost-effective because they don't use overwhelming amounts of advertising offers. Also, micro- and nano-influencers typically use revolutionary platforms like TikTok and Instagram. It means, when you partner with them, you have the chance to tap a higher market share.

- **Cross-device tracking:** This is the latest technology that tracks the same users' activities across multiple devices, such as smartphones and smart TVs (Cross-Device Tracking, 2023). Nowadays, many use mobile phones to shop online. Therefore, this is an essential feature that you must maintain across all the platforms to provide a seamless buyer experience from start to finish.

- **In-app monitoring and attribution:** As I indicated in the previous section, mobile application usage has increased over the past years. Over 50% of affiliate traffic comes from mobile users (Geyser, 2023). So, this technique is useful to track user behavior throughout the funnel (from user clicks to conversions) and identify the areas for improvement and where users are dropping off your sales process.

   Many affiliate networks have partnered with mobile measurement partners (MMPs), and they organize, calculate, and regulate app user events and data. The good thing is, most of the ecommerce apps already come with an MMP.

- **Voice and virtual searches:** Augmented reality-based browsing plus live social media shopping became more popular in 2022, and around 27% of online users use voice or virtual search when browsing products or services (Geyser, 2023). So, it's better to focus more on visual- and audio-based content than text-based. TikTok's live shopping feature is a great example of this method.

- **Discontinuation of third-party cookies:** As you already know, cookies are an integral technology that records and tracks customer behavior. However, in 2021, Google announced the discontinuation of third-party cookies. Since then, many marketers have used AI-powered tools, social listening, on-page analytics, and conversational marketing to gather customer insights and stay on the right track with brand engagement.

- **Promoting cryptocurrencies and non-fungible tokens:** Now, you can promote certain types of cryptocurrencies, non-fungible tokens, or a platform and help reach a wider audience.

Apart from these prominent trends, we can see there are more diverse affiliate marketers for advertisers, and more competition for brands and affiliate marketers than before. Furthermore, there is more community-based affiliate marketing and loyalty marketing as positive trends in the field. Before we move to the conclusion, I would like to give you a small tip based on my personal experiences.

Remember, opportunities don't just come. You have to seek them. Always keep up with trends and research the market. That's the best possible way to open up new opportunities. Try this technique for some time. You will be overwhelmed by the abundance of opportunities you have to grow your affiliate marketing business.

Conclusion

Here is a summary of the crucial factors we discussed in each chapter. Also, you can utilize this summary to identify any areas that you might have missed. Let's begin with the first chapter. As an affiliate marketer, you earn a commission when consumers purchase products or services via your affiliate link.

Affiliate marketing is a great source of passive income, and it provides further income opportunities as well. Flexibility, low risk, low cost, and easy to execute are the advantages of affiliate marketing. Additionally, affiliate marketing is a great way to drive traffic to websites, social media, and blogs.

High competition, commission-based payouts, and possible fraudulent activities are the main disadvantages of affiliate marketing. Overall, affiliate marketing is a good choice to earn an extra income. Merchants, affiliate marketers, consumers, and affiliate networks are the main element of affiliate marketing. Unattached, related, and involved are the main types of affiliate marketing. It's your own decision to select the method you prefer but the involved method is the most ethical approach to doing affiliate marketing.

Let's go through the steps of building your affiliate marketing strategy. The first step is researching a suitable niche. Start analyzing your interests, skills, passion, and strengths. Based on that, list the potential niches where you could start affiliate marketing as a business.

For example, if you're passionate about gardening, you may start promoting gardening   equipment   and tools since you have sound knowledge and capabilities in that particular area. Then, analyze whether your interests meet customers' demands and solve their problems in that niche. Next, analyze the profitability, competition, search volume, and traffic sources of certain niches.

Choosing a suitable niche is sometimes daunting because it requires a lot of patience and hard work. Still, it's a kind of mandatory task you have to fulfill before moving ahead with other steps. Think, choosing the right niche is like a long-term investment. So, take time and research more to make a worthwhile decision.

As the second step, you have to choose the right platform according to your niche's preferences. Websites, social media, YouTube, newsletters, and podcasts are the most popular platforms for affiliate marketing.

The third step is building an audience around your affiliate marketing campaign. Analyze competitors and traffic to have a bigger picture of your target audience. Most importantly, be trustworthy with your audience, and stay relevant with your content to improve the authority of your affiliate marketing campaign. Paid promotion is a good way to promote your content, so engage with the current audience and acquire more visitors.

The fourth step is signing up for an appropriate affiliate program. By signing a partnership with an affiliate program, you agree to promote your partner's products or services, and they agree to pay you a commission for that. Search affiliates, influencer programs, review sites, coupon sites, and email marketing are the main types of affiliate programs.

As we identified in Chapter 6, Amazon Associates, Rakuten, Shopify, eBay Partner Network, Semrush, Leadpages, and HubSpot are the most famous affiliate programs available in the market. To find the most suitable affiliate program according to your niche, first analyze the background information of the affiliate program to check whether they have a good reputation. You then choose a product that you have used before and make sure to promote the products that fit your niche.

It's better to settle with an affiliate program that offers high commission rates. Before you sign up, don't forget to analyze payment methods, payment threshold, cookie life, and terms and conditions. Also, cross-check with affiliate program owners to see whether they provide enough support, an affiliate kit, and a system to track sales.

Choosing the right product to promote is the fifth step. As I highlighted many times, pick a product that you've used before, and that fits within your niche.

Creating remarkable content is the sixth step. Product review comparisons, roundups, tutorials, emails, ebooks, landing pages, case studies, resource pages, how-to articles, listicles, guides, and seasonal content are the most common content types that can be used in affiliate marketing. Always try your best to publish unique and quality content. Here is a checklist for remarkable content.

- Would your target audience share it?

- Does it contain original data?

- Does it offer a unique perspective on a topic?

- Is the way you present information different from the norm?

- Is it timely?

- Is the idea conveyed in a way that is easy to understand?

- Does the overall content exemplify a high-quality standard?

There are plenty of free tools available for content research, content writing, editing, designing, and productivity. Do not forget to utilize them to produce outstanding content.

In Chapter 5, we mainly focused on how to build momentum and achieve sustainability in affiliate marketing based on five steps. Keep in mind, this is the second part of building your own affiliate marketing strategy.

The seventh step is driving traffic to your affiliate site.

In the eighth step, you have to think about how to get more clicks for your affiliate links.

Link placement, context, and callouts are the critical factors you must take into account to get the maximum benefit from affiliate links. It's a great idea to use different methods to promote links; for example, underlining hyperlinks or adding affiliate links in your navigation menus.

As the ninth step, we discuss how to track your affiliate campaigns. You may use different tracking methods, live reporting, and analytics tools to evaluate the results of the affiliate campaign. This is an essential step to correct your errors and take immediate steps for further improvement of the affiliate marketing strategy.

Cookies, SubID tracking systems, per-product tracking, and impression tracking are the main types of affiliate marketing tracking methods, and affiliate marketing software is an advanced tool to analyze traffic and conversions.

As the 10th step, we discuss multiple strategies for maximizing sales. This is an important step to successfully running your affiliate campaign in the long run. Linking to conversion-optimized landing pages, highlighting reviews, repurposing content, and adding new merchants are a few of the methods that you can use to increase your sales. As the final step, you must check how you get paid for your effort, whether it's based on sales, leads, or clicks.

In Chapter 6, I discussed some real-life examples. I hope it helps you to understand how people use different techniques to earn money as well as build their audience. In the previous chapter, we focused on the mistakes to avoid, tips, and current trends. Conversely, I believe your tendency to make mistakes will be reduced because now you have an idea of the possible mistakes. Use the tips and trends we discussed to develop a new affiliate marketing strategy or to enhance your existing one.

Pat Flynn once mentioned, "Affiliate marketing is not a 'push-button' solution. It takes focus and commitment, and a certain choreography to make it happen the way you want it to" (Convertful, 2019). There you have it! You won't be able to see the results of your effort overnight.

Your continuous time commitment, hard work, and patience are required to highlight your name as a successful affiliate marketer one day. Therefore, each step, stage, and tiny piece of information we discussed earlier plays a huge role in your affiliate marketing journey. Therefore, no matter what, don't skip or miss any of them.

Every single day, we experience something new. Who knows whether it's an opportunity for you? So, think differently and be innovative. Unlike three to four decades back, you now have huge potential to become successful in affiliate marketing. I strongly believe the knowledge you gained from this book will guide you on the right path! Good luck, and I hope you achieve fantastic results.

Thank you for reading this book, and I would really appreciate it if you could share your valuable feedback.

References

Adtraction. (n.d.). *9 things to consider when choosing an affiliate network.* https://adtraction.com/articles/9-things-to-consider-when-choosing-an-affiliate-network

Advertise Purple. (2020, January 18). *15 frequently asked questions about affiliate marketing.* https://www.advertisepurple.com/15-frequently-asked-questions-about-affiliate-marketing/

Anjani, N. (2022, August 12). *How to start affiliate marketing: 9 steps to a successful affiliate marketing business.* Hostinger Tutorials. https://www.hostinger.com/tutorials/how-to-start-affiliate-marketing

Baker, K. (2019). *The ultimate guide to influencer marketing in 2019.* HubSpot. https://blog.hubspot.com/marketing/how-to-work-with-influencers

Bari, S. (2019, May 13). *The pros & cons of affiliate marketing | A practical overview.* WP Manage Ninja. https://wpmanageninja.com/pros-and-cons-of-affiliate-marketing/

Becker, B. (2018). *Image alt text: What it is, how to write it, and why it matters to SEO.* HubSpot. https://blog.hubspot.com/marketing/image-alt-text

BigCommerce. (2022, April 25). *Affiliate marketing 101: What it is and how to get started.* https://www.bigcommerce.com/articles/ecommerce/affiliate-marketing/

Blain, B. (2022, September 8). *6 best social media platforms for affiliate marketing.* Printify.com. https://printify.com/blog/best-social-media-platforms-for-affiliate-marketing/

Chukwudi, C. (2021, March 24). *8 things you must know before signing up for an affiliate program.* Jeffbullas's Blog. https://www.jeffbullas.com/signing-up-for-an-affiliate-program/

Convertful. (2019, April 26). *120 marketing quotes to get inspired.* https://convertful.com/marketing-quotes/#10_Affiliate_Marketing_Quotes

Costa, J. (2021, August 24). *How to start affiliate marketing in 2023 (7 simple steps).* Affilimate. https://affilimate.com/blog/affiliate-marketing/

Cox, L. K. (2023, February 23). *45 free content writing tools to love [for writing, editing & content creation].* HubSpot. https://blog.hubspot.com/marketing/free-content-marketing-tools-list

Csizmadia, A. (2021, August 3). *How to launch an affiliate email marketing campaign.* Post Affiliate Pro. https://www.postaffiliatepro.com/blog/how-to-launch-an-affiliate-email-marketing-campaign/

Diggity Marketing. (2019, November 4). *15 best affiliate networks of 2022: The year's top platforms.* https://diggitymarketing.com/best-affiliate-networks/

Digital Scholar. (2022, July 5). *The pros and cons of affiliate marketing in 2022.* https://digitalscholar.in/pros-and-cons-of-affiliate-marketing/

Dynamic Yield. (n.d.). *Social proof.* https://www.dynamicyield.com/glossary/social-proof/

Editorial Team. (2019, October 17). *11 awesome affiliate marketing tracking software.* Bit Blog. https://blog.bit.ai/affiliate-marketing-tracking-software/

Editorial Team. (2022, August 16). *How to create an affiliate marketing website in 9 easy steps.* Astra. https://wpastra.com/guides-and-tutorials/how-to-create-affiliate-marketing-website/

Faisal, S. (2021, May 24). *How do I start blogging for affiliate marketing | 6 steps 2021.* LinkedIn. https://www.linkedin.com/pulse/how-do-i-start-blogging-affiliate-marketing-6-steps-2021-faisal/

Fat Stacks. (2016, November 22). *25 clever ways to get more clicks on affiliate links.* https://fatstacksblog.com/more-affiliate-link-clicks/

Finance Magnates Staff. (2023, February 8). *What challenges do affiliate marketers face in 2023?* Finance Magnates. https://www.financemagnates.com/forex/technology/what-challenges-do-affiliate-marketers-face-in-2023/

Flynn, P. (2018, October 8). *3 types of affiliate marketing explained—and the one I profit from.* Smart Passive Income. https://www.smartpassiveincome.com/blog/3-types-of-affiliate-marketing-explained-and-the-one-i-profit-from/

Forsey, C. (2021, March 1). *What is content writing? Plus 12 tips to take your content to the next level.* HubSpot. https://blog.hubspot.com/marketing/professional-content-mistakes

Forsey, C. (2022, December 22). *The beginner's guide to setting up a blog.* HubSpot. https://blog.hubspot.com/marketing/how-to-set-up-blog

Frankenfield, J. (2022, October 22). *Affiliate marketer: Definition, examples, and how to get started.* Investopedia.

https://www.investopedia.com/terms/a/affiliat
e-marketing.asp#toc-types-of-affiliate-
marketing

Freund, D. (2023, March 30). *7 common mistakes every affiliate marketer needs to avoid.* Intergrowth. https://intergrowth.com/affiliate-
marketing/mistakes/

GCFGlobal.org. (2019). *Money basics: Financial problem-solving strategies.* https://edu.gcfglobal.org/en/moneybasics/fina
ncial-problem-solving-strategies/1/

Geyser, W. (2023, February 28). *Affiliate marketing trends you need to know in 2023.* Refersion. https://www.refersion.com/blog/affiliate-
marketing-trends/

Grabijas, E. (2019, February 20). *25 affiliate marketing FAQs for marketing managers.* Awin. https://www.awin.com/us/how-to-use-
awin/25-questions-about-affiliate-marketing

Grabijas, E. (2019, March 25). *How to generate affiliate marketing traffic for your offers.* Awin. https://www.awin.com/us/how-to-use-
awin/nine-great-ways-to-generate-traffic-for-
your-affiliate-offers

GRIN Contributor. (2021, December 22). *Affiliate marketing vs influencer marketing | grin.* Grin.co. https://grin.co/blog/affiliate-marketing-vs-
influencer-marketing/

Hart, M. (2023, January 2). *The 5-step process for finding your business's ideal niche market.* HubSpot. https://blog.hubspot.com/sales/niche-market

Hayes, M. (2022, January 20). *What is affiliate marketing? A 2022 guide to getting started.* Shopify. https://www.shopify.com/blog/affiliate-marketing

Hollatz, K. (2018, May 1). *How to choose which affiliate products to sell to your readers.* ConvertKit. https://convertkit.com/resources/blog/how-to-start-affiliate-marketing

Hollatz, K. (n.d.). *How to start affiliate marketing: A dead-simple guide.* ConvertKit. https://convertkit.com/resources/guides/how-to-start-affiliate-marketing

HubSpot. (n.d.). *Campaign assistant: HubSpot's free AI marketing asset creator.* https://www.hubspot.com/campaign-assistant

Hughes, J. (2022, December 13). *How to create a website for affiliate marketing (in 8 steps).* Themeisle Blog. https://themeisle.com/blog/how-to-create-a-website-for-affiliate-marketing/#gref

Hughes, J. (2022, October 11). *How to create a loyal audience with affiliate marketing (3 tips).* Easy Affiliate. https://easyaffiliate.com/blog/loyal-audience-affiliate-marketing/

146

Huhn, J. (2020, November 20). *11 affiliate marketing examples to inspire your own program.* Referral Rock. https://referralrock.com/blog/affiliate-program-examples/

Hunt, M. (2017, March 24). *Top 10 affiliate marketing tracking software platforms.* Entrepreneur. https://www.entrepreneur.com/growing-a-business/top-10-affiliate-marketing-tracking-software-platforms/291042

Iskiev, M. (2023). *The fastest growing social media platforms of 2023 [New data].* HubSpot. https://blog.hubspot.com/marketing/fastest-growing-social-media-platforms

Juviler, J. (2022, June 7). *14 best social media widgets for WordPress in 2022.* HubSpot. https://blog.hubspot.com/website/10-best-free-social-sharing-button-widgets-2018

Keenan, M. (2022a, February 1). *How to start affiliate marketing with no money.* Shopify. https://www.shopify.com/blog/start-affiliate-marketing-with-no-money

Keenan, M. (2022b, November 22). *25+ affiliate programs to help you earn money (2022).* Shopify. https://www.shopify.com/blog/best-affiliate-programs

Kinsta. (2023a, February 14). *Affiliate link cloaking – How to do it in WordPress (2 different ways).*

https://kinsta.com/affiliate-academy/link-cloaking/

Kinsta. (2023b, May 11). *21 proven tips to increase your affiliate sales in 2022.* https://kinsta.com/affiliate-academy/affiliate-sales-tips/

Korsten, H. (n.d.). *How to build an email list for affiliate marketing.* Supermetrics.com. https://supermetrics.com/blog/how-to-build-an-email-list-for-affiliate-marketing

Kurcwald, K. (2022, June 27). *15 types of affiliate marketing content to promote products.* NapoleonCat. https://napoleoncat.com/blog/affiliate-marketing-content/

Lee, J. (2021, March 18). *Affiliate marketing for beginners: What you need to know.* HubSpot. https://blog.hubspot.com/marketing/affiliate-marketing-guidek

Leist, R. (2019). *How to write a blog post: a step-by-step guide [+ free blog post templates].* HubSpot. https://blog.hubspot.com/marketing/how-to-start-a-blog

Lent, M. (2021, October 23). *12 best ways to promote affiliate links.* Affilimate. https://affilimate.com/blog/promote-affiliate-links/

Linda D. (2022, August 10). *15 affiliate marketing tips to increase your income in 2023.* Hostinger Tutorials. https://www.hostinger.com/tutorials/affiliate-marketing-tips

Marinaki, A. (2021, April 23). *80 glorious marketing quotes to empower and inspire you.* Moosend. https://moosend.com/blog/marketing-quotes/

Markopoulou, E. (2022, April 15). *How to choose the right affiliate program.* Coupler.io Blog. https://blog.coupler.io/how-to-choose-the-right-affiliate-program/#How_a_perfect_affiliate_program_should_look_like

McGinley, C. (2022, September 15). *Influencer marketing strategy checklist & template.* HubSpot. https://blog.hubspot.com/marketing/influencer-marketing-power

Mendpara, J. (2022, June 29). *13 inspiring affiliate marketing program examples.* Social Snowball. https://blog.socialsnowball.io/affiliate-marketing-program-examples/

Mileva, G. (2021, December 29). *The ultimate list of affiliate marketing statistics for 2022.* Influencer Marketing Hub. https://influencermarketinghub.com/affiliate-marketing-stats/

Mileva, G. (2023, June 20). *Top 7 affiliate marketing trends for 2023.* Influencer Marketing Hub.

https://influencermarketinghub.com/affiliate-marketing-trends/#toc-2

Militaru, D. (2022, June 23). *Best 11 traffic sources for affiliate marketing*. The 2Checkout Blog. https://blog.2checkout.com/best-traffic-sources-for-affiliate-marketing/

Namecheap. (n.d.). *10 steps to affiliate marketing success*. https://www.namecheap.com/affiliates/10-steps-affiliate-marketing-success/

Needle, F. (2022, November 18). *Benefits of influencer marketing [Data + expert insight]*. HubSpot. https://blog.hubspot.com/marketing/benefits-of-influencer-marketing

Oberlo. (2023). *How many people use email in 2023?* [Feb 2023 Update]. https://www.oberlo.com/statistics/how-many-people-use-email

Oklahoma Central Credit Union. (n.d.). *Ten common financial challenges*. https://www.oklahomacentral.creditunion/Ten-Common-Financial-Challenges

Ong, S. Q. (2020, January 16). *Affiliate marketing for beginners: 7 steps to success*. Ahrefs Blog. https://ahrefs.com/blog/affiliate-marketing/

Palmer, W. (2022, June 13). *How to grow your affiliate marketing email list (in 2023)*. AffiliateWP.

https://affiliatewp.com/affiliate-marketing-email-list/

Patel, N. (2015). *Affiliate marketing made simple: A step-by-step guide.* Neil Patel. https://neilpatel.com/what-is-affiliate-marketing/

Patel, N. (2017, September 7). *How to find a profitable niche in affiliate marketing.* Neil Patel. https://neilpatel.com/blog/find-profitable-niche-affiliate-marketing/

Patel, N. (2020, December 30). *The top affiliate marketing networks.* Neil Patel. https://neilpatel.com/blog/affiliate-marketing-networks/

Pat Will Help U. (2022, January 15). *What do microsites have to do with affiliate marketing?* https://patwillhelpu.com/what-do-microsites-have-to-do-with-affiliate-marketing/

Pitre, A. (2021, June 22). *29 simple ways to grow your email list.* HubSpot. https://blog.hubspot.com/blog/tabid/6307/bid/32028/25-clever-ways-to-grow-your-email-marketing-list.aspx

Profitable Freelancer. (2022, March 27). *How to start an affiliate blog the right way.* https://www.profitablefreelancer.com/how-to-start-an-affiliate-blog-the-right-way

Rangel, J. (2020, May 27). *How to use social media for affiliate marketing.* Optinmonster. https://optinmonster.com/how-to-use-social-media-for-affiliate-marketing/

Rastas, J. (n.d.-a). *Influencer affiliate marketing: How influencers can grow your affiliate program.* Supermetrics.com. https://supermetrics.com/blog/influencer-affiliate-marketing

Rastas, J. (n.d.-b). *Top 10 affiliate marketing mistakes.* Supermetrics. https://supermetrics.com/blog/top-10-affiliate-marketing-mistakes

Roche, N. (2021, September 6). *16 best affiliate marketing programs for beginners in 2023.* Authority Hacker. https://www.authorityhacker.com/best-affiliate-programs-beginners/

Rogers, M. (2022, February 20). *Affiliate product selection - 7 tips for pinpointing the perfect product.* Affiliate Marketer Training. https://www.affiliatemarketertraining.com/affiliate-product-selection/

Ruby, D. (2022, November 5). *YouTube statistics (2022) — Updated data, facts & figures shared!* Demand Sage. https://www.demandsage.com/youtube-stats/

Ruby, D. (2023, March 29). *73+ affiliate marketing statistics 2023 (Data & infographics).* DemandSage.

https://www.demandsage.com/affiliate-marketing-statistics/

Saint-Juste, D. (2023, April 6). *44 of the best affiliate programs that pay the highest commission.* HubSpot. https://blog.hubspot.com/marketing/best-affiliate-programs

Santos, A. B. (n.d.). *How to reach more people when affiliate marketing.* SoftwareKeep. https://softwarekeep.com/help-center/how-to-reach-more-people-when-affiliate-marketing

Sharm, S. (2022, May 3). *How to use social media in affiliate marketing (7 essential tips).* Smash Balloon. https://smashballoon.com/social-media-affiliate-marketing-essential-tips/

Shawn, S. (2020, December 2). *7 ways to find a profitable niche for affiliate marketing.* AAWP. https://getaawp.com/blog/finding-a-profitable-niche-affiliate-marketing/#4_Gauge_the_Number_of_Traffic_Sources_Available

Sid, M. (2022, September 4). *How to approach influencers for affiliate marketing.* AFLUENCER. https://afluencer.com/how-approach-influencers-affiliate-marketing/

Smart Passive Income. (n.d.). *Affiliate marketing - How to increase your income by recommending products and services.*

https://www.smartpassiveincome.com/guide/affiliate-marketing-strategies/

Szuchan, S. (2022, November 30). *How to create a blog for affiliate marketing that makes cash (2023).* SamSzu.com. https://samszu.com/how-to-create-a-blog-for-affiliate-marketing/

ThemeDev Inc. (2022, July 23). *How to create an email list for affiliate marketing.* LinkedIn. https://www.linkedin.com/pulse/how-create-email-list-affiliate-marketing-themedev/

Thrasher, D. (2023, January 6). *How to drive traffic to affiliate links: 9 tips for 2023!* ClickBank.https://www.clickbank.com/blog/how-to-drive-traffic-to-affiliate-links/

Torres, J. (2022, August 19). *10 biggest mistakes in affiliate marketing to avoid.* JonTorres. https://jontorres.com/mistakes-in-affiliate-marketing/

Trackdesk Team. (2023, January 12). *Affiliate tracking: Everything you must know in 2023.* Trackdesk.com. https://trackdesk.com/blog/affiliate-tracking-everything-you-must-know

Triantafyllopoulou, N. (2022, June 22). *The biggest affiliate marketing trends in 2023.* Coupler.io Blog. https://blog.coupler.io/affiliate-marketing-trends/

Vaughan, P. (2016, October 20). *The ultimate 8-point checklist for remarkable content.* HubSpot. https://blog.hubspot.com/blog/tabid/6307/bid/18476/the-ultimate-8-point-checklist-for-remarkable-content.aspx

Widmer, B. (2023, April 11). *7 affiliate marketing examples & why they work so well.* Ahrefs Blog. https://ahrefs.com/blog/affiliate-marketing-examples/

WordStream. (n.d.). *What is anchor text?* https://www.wordstream.com/anchor-text

Zaballa, R. (2023, March 6). *10 affiliate marketing examples for a successful affiliate program.* Penji. https://penji.co/affiliate-marketing-examples/

Printed in Great Britain
by Amazon

37223680R00096